**Serving Award-Winning Lowcountry
Cuisine Since 1982**

Lowcountry Cooking with 82 Queen

by
Stephen G. Kish, Chef Proprietor, C.E.C.

Lowcountry humor and historic highlights
by Patra Bucher

Wentworth Printing
Columbia, South Carolina

Published by Wentworth Printing
Columbia, South Carolina

© 2006 82 Queen, Inc.
All rights reserved.

Lowcountry Cooking with Eighty-Two Queen
ISBN 0-9713841-1-8

In Appreciation

In every kitchen and in every restaurant, there is a person in charge: the chef. A chef is only as good as his fellow chefs, sous chefs, and cooks. We would like to dedicate this cookbook to all the chefs and cooks who have been part of 82 Queen since it opened in April 1982. Without the hard work of these fine culinarians, 82 Queen would not be the caliber of restaurant we have today.

Stephen G. Kish, C.E.C.
Chef/Proprietor

Brad Jones
Executive Chef

Our special thanks to:

Andy Allen	Mark Miramontes
Jon Banta	Billy Mitchell
Darby Boston	Mark Nicholas
Gerald Bunkham	Kevin Powell
Chad Cambell	Tim Price
Jassen Campbell	Brad Register
Jennifer Cohen	Kevin Riera
Morgan Cryster	Jeff Roots
Ben Culp	Kevin Shirley
Johnny Floresta	Chris Speicher
Steve Greene	Steve Stone
Greg Jenkins	Keith Taylor
Ricky Jenkins	Brooks Vaughn
Steven Lusby	James Washington
Enoch McCue	Janson Yuhasz
Kathleen McNeil	Dillon Zenobi

Contents

7 Appetizers, Relishes & Chutneys

29 Salads, Dressings & Vegetables

47 Grits, Rice, Pasta & Bread

62 Soups, Stocks & Sauces

87 Seafood

104 Meat & Fowl

116 The Perfect Pair Recipe

144 Desserts

165 Cocktails

174 82 Queen Merchandise & Condiments

Appetizers, Relishes & Chutneys

Lowcountry Cooking with 82 Queen

Appetizers

Cabbage-Wrapped Lump Crabmeat ... 10
Chilled Scallops in Sour Cream & Shallot Sauce ... 11
Clams à la Queen ... 12
Corn Crêpe ... 12
Cornbread Oysters ... 13
Crab Dip ... 14
Crab Spinach Dip ... 14
Grilled Clams with Garlic Chive Butter ...15
Oyster Fritters ... 15
Oysters Baked with Watercress and Saffron Bacon Butter ... 16
Oysters Elizabeth ... 17
Oysters on the Half Shell with Avocado Salsa ... 18
Seafood Sausage ... 19
Shrimp Crisp ... 19
Shrimp Griddle Cakes ... 19
Wasabi Fried Oysters with Lowcountry Pepper Sauce ... 20

Relishes

82 Queen Deli Pickles ... 21
Black-Eyed Pea Relish ... 21
Caper Relish ... 22
Corn Relish ... 22
Cranberry Relish ... 22
Pineapple Relish ... 23
Red Pepper Jelly ... 23
Roasted Corn & Tomato Relish ... 24
Tomato Jalapeño Salsa ... 24

Chutneys

Apple & Orange Chutney ... 25
Apple Mint Chutney ... 25
Apple or Pear Chutney ... 26
Cranberry & Gold Raisin Chutney ... 26
Fig Chutney ... 26
Kiwi Chutney ... 27
Pineapple-Mango Chutney ... 27

Cabbage-Wrapped Lump Crabmeat

8	leaves green cabbage, membrane removed
1 lb.	fresh jumbo lump crabmeat, well picked
1 tsp.	fresh dill weed
1 Tbsp.	lemon juice
2 tsp.	margarine
	Dash of salt and pepper
	Water for poaching

Pre-heat oven to 400°. Bring water to a boil and poach cabbage until limp. Refresh in ice-cold water. Spread cabbage on flat surface. Place crabmeat in center of cabbage and top with dill, lemon juice, margarine, salt, and pepper. Fold two ends together and then fold other two ends to the center to make a square pocket. Bake at 400° for 10 minutes.

Yield: 8 (4 oz.) serving

Chilled Scallops in Sour Cream & Shallot Sauce

1 lb.	(30–40 count) sea scallops, fresh
2 cups	sour cream
1 cup	mayonnaise
¼ cup	lemon juice
1 Tbsp.	salt
1 tsp.	dry mustard
3 Tbsp.	shallots, chopped
3 Tbsp.	fresh chives or dill, chopped

Lightly poach scallops in salted water until barely done. Check by cutting one scallop in half (it should be white in the center). Be careful not to overcook as it will make them tough. Drain and cool. In a mixing bowl, combine all remaining ingredients and mix well. Add scallops and let them marinate for at least 3 hours. Serve on a bed of any type of lettuce or greens.

Yield: 6–8 appetizer servings.

Clams à la Queen

20 Littleneck clams, shucked and on the half shell
Queen mixture
Bacon bits
Parsley sprig
Lemon

Cook bacon bits. Top clams on the half shell with Queen mixture and cooked bacon bits. Place on oyster dish and bake at 325° until piping hot (about 15 minutes). Serve with lemon wedge and parsley garnish. Can be served on rock salt.

Queen Mixture

1 cup pimentos, diced
1 large onion, diced
2 green peppers, diced
1/2 lb. mushrooms, diced
Garlic butter

Sauté onions and peppers in garlic butter; cool and add pimento and raw diced mushrooms.

Yield: 4 appetizer servings.

Corn Crêpe

12 eggs
1 cup milk
1 1/2 cups flour
2 cups cornmeal
2 tsp. salt
1/4 cup scallions
1 cup chopped canned corn, drained well
1/4 cup sugar
1 Tbsp. cayenne
1 jalapeño pepper

Mix eggs and milk together. Add remaining ingredients and let stand 20 minutes before using. Crêpes can be filled with pulled BBQ duck or seafood. Great as an appetizer or an entrée.

Yield: 20 crêpes.

Cornbread Oysters

24	fresh oysters
2	pieces of cornbread
1/2 cup	breadcrumbs
1/2 cup	flour
2	eggs
1/4 cup	milk
1 Tbsp.	chopped bacon, cooked
1 cup	black bean sauce
1 cup	smoked tomato sauce
1/4 cup	sour cream
	Salt and pepper to taste

Shuck fresh oysters. Set up three bowls for breading. In the first bowl add flour, salt, and pepper. In the second bowl mix the eggs and milk. In the third bowl crumble the cornbread and the breadcrumbs. Dip the oysters in the flour, then the egg mixture, and then in cornbread mixture. Lightly pan-fry the oysters. Spread the sauces and the sour cream on the bottom of the plate and arrange the oysters on top. Sprinkle with bacon.

Yield: 4 appetizer servings.

Eating Out is Good for Your Health

The word "restaurant" comes from the French word for "restoration." In the 18th century, specialized shops in France began serving broth and boullion, considered to be restorative to one's health. Tables were later added, transforming these shops into restaurants. The first true restaurant was actually opened in Paris in 1760.

APPETIZERS, RELISHES & CHUTNEYS

Crab Dip

1 lb.	cream cheese, room temperature
1/4 cup	sour cream
1 lb.	special crabmeat, picked
1/2 cup	shredded Cheddar
	Pinch white pepper
1 Tbsp.	Worcestershire sauce
2 Tbsp.	horseradish
4	green onions, chopped fine
1/2 tsp.	salt

Mix all ingredients together. Dip can be prepared the day before it is needed and will keep one week in the refrigerator.

Yield: 12 large servings.

Crab-Spinach Dip

1 lb.	cream cheese, room temperature
1 lb.	crab, special
4	green onions, chopped fine
1 Tbsp.	horseradish, squeezed
1/2 Tbsp.	salt
1 oz.	lemon juice
1/2 cup	mayonnaise
1/2 lb.	spinach, picked, and wilted in white wine

Combine all ingredients until smooth. Bake in dish for 10 minutes at 350° or until brown and bubbling.

Yield: 12 servings.

Grilled Clams with Garlic-Chive Butter

    12   cherrystone clams
           Garlic-Chive butter

Open fresh clams with clam knife. Discard top halves of the shells. Stuff clams with 1 teaspoon of garlic-chive butter. Place clams on hot open face gas or charcoal grill. Cook until butter is melted and bubbling hot.

Garlic-Chive Butter

      1 lb.   butter, softened to room temperature
    1/4 cup   fresh chives, chopped
        1   lemon (juice only)
    1 Tbsp.   fresh garlic, chopped
  1 1/2 tsp.   salt
    1/2 tsp.   white pepper

Mix all ingredients in mixing bowl by hand or with electric mixer. Store in airtight container. Keeps up to 3 weeks.

                              Yield: 2 appetizer servings.

Oyster Fritters

     1 qt.   oysters, drained well and chopped
    1 cup   corn meal
    1 cup   all-purpose flour
       2   eggs
  1 Tbsp.   baking powder
  1/4 cup   scallions, diced
     1/4   red pepper, diced and rinsed
  1/2 cup   Half & Half cream
    1 tsp.   Cajun seasoning
    1 tsp.   fresh thyme, chopped
    1 oz.   shrimp base

In large bowl, combine all ingredients except oysters. Mix well. Add oysters last, folding in gently. Drop spoonfuls into 350° oil and fry until golden brown.

                              Yield: 4–6 servings.

Oysters Baked with Watercress and Saffron-Bacon Butter

  12 fresh oysters on the half shell
  2 bunches fresh watercress
1/4 cup pine nuts, chopped
1/2 cup bread crumbs
    Saffron-Bacon butter

Open oysters with an oyster knife and loosen from shell. Lightly poach watercress. Lace oyster with watercress, then top with saffron-bacon butter. Bake at 350° for 2 minutes. Top with pine nuts and breadcrumbs. Bake for another 3 minutes.

Saffron-Bacon Butter

1/2 lb. butter
  1 small shallot
1/4 cup chopped bacon
1/4 cup white wine
1/4 cup lemon juice
1/2 g. saffron
1 tsp. garlic, chopped
1/2 tsp. lemon rind
    White pepper and salt to taste

Whip butter and set aside. Simmer shallots and garlic in wine and lemon juice mixture until reduced by one-half. Let cool, then add to whipped butter. Add bacon, saffron, lemon rind, salt and pepper.

               Yield: 2 appetizer servings.

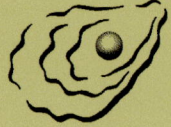

A Historic Pearl

If you love oysters, you've come to the right place. In season, oysters are practically a Charleston staple. In fact, White Point Gardens, also known as the Battery, got its name from the large mounds of white oysters shells that once covered the point of Charleston's peninsula. They were present in such large quantities that crushed oyster shells once made up the streets and sidewalks of Charleston.

Oysters Elizabeth

First Place Winner, Oyster Recipe Contest

12	oysters, on the half shell
1	cup fresh spinach, cooked and chopped
1/2 cup	white crabmeat
1/4 cup	sautéed onion, chopped fine
1/4 cup	cracker meal
3 tsp.	mayonnaise
1/2 tsp.	dry mustard
1 tsp.	Worcestershire sauce
1 tsp.	lemon juice
	Dash of Tabasco sauce
	Salt and pepper to taste
	Melted butter

Blanch spinach in boiling water 10 seconds. Drain and chop. Add all remaining ingredients (except oysters and butter), tossing gently. Stuff oysters and top with melted butter. Bake at 400° for 5–7 minutes. Serve with lemon and cocktail sauce.

Yield: 2 appetizer servings.

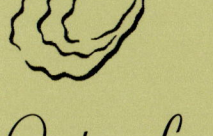

Oyster Love

Science has uncovered little evidence to support the claim, so how oysters came to be championed as an aphrodisiac is unclear. Nevertheless, many cultures believe that an oyster is as potent as powdered rhinoceros horn, but a lot better tasting. A culinary favorite for thousands of years, oyster meat varies in color from creamy beige to pale gray, in flavor from bland to salty, and in texture from tender to firm. Casanova reportedly ate 50 or more salty ones before each of his evening's conquests. What about sex lives of oysters? Interestingly, oysters possess both male and female sex organs.

APPETIZERS, RELISHES & CHUTNEYS

Oysters on the Half Shell with Avocado Salsa

  4 dozen oysters on the half shell, raw
   15 strips bacon, diced and cooked until crisp, drained well and crumbled
     Avocado salsa

This is a cold appetizer served with the oysters raw. Arrange oysters, topping each with salsa and bacon.

Avocado Salsa

    4 medium tomatoes, peeled, seeded, chopped fine
   1/2 medium green bell pepper, minced fine
    3 scallions, minced fine
 1 1/2 tsp. garlic, mashed to purée form
    1 lemon (juice only)
  1/2 tsp. salt
  1/4 tsp. black pepper
 3 to 6 dashes of Tabasco sauce
    1 large ripe avocado, peeled, diced fine

Mix all ingredients in a stainless steel mixing bowl. Refrigerate 30 minutes.

Yield: 8 appetizer servings.

Seafood Sausage

  1/4 lb. shrimp
  1/4 lb. scallops
  1/4 lb. white flaky fish
    1 egg
  1/4 cup heavy cream
  1 tsp. salt
  1/2 tsp. white pepper
  1/4 tsp. cayenne
  2 Tbsp. fresh herbs to include parsley, dill, and basil
    1 large sausage casing

Purée shrimp, scallops, and fish in food processor. Add egg, cream, and spices, blending well. Place mixture into pastry bag with round tip. Put sausage casing on round pastry bag tip and fill casing with puréed seafood mixture; twist casing every 3 inches to portion sausages. Tie ends with knot. Place sausage in pot. Cover with water and season with salt, pepper, and lemon. Bring to a simmer and cook for 5 minutes. Remove sausage from pot and let cool. Sausage can be grilled or baked.

Yield: 6 sausages.

Shrimp Crisp

12	wonton wraps (3x3 in.)
24	large shrimp
2 pt.	bean sprouts, chopped
2	small shallots, diced
¼ lb.	butter or margarine
2	eggs
1 qt.	frying shortening
	Salt and pepper to taste

Peel and dice shrimp. In medium size sauté pan, melt butter and sauté shrimp until they turn pink. Add shallots and sprouts and sauté quickly for 2–3 minutes. Set mixture aside and let cool. Lay out wonton wraps and divide shrimp mixture between them. Brush edges of wonton wrap with egg and fold one time. Be sure edges are sealed completely. Let sit for 20 minutes. Heat shortening to 350° and fry wontons until golden brown.

Yield: 6 appetizer servings.

Shrimp Griddle Cakes

4	eggs
8 oz.	Half & Half cream
1 cup	corn meal
1½ cups	flour
1 tsp.	baking powder
½ tsp.	cayenne
1 oz.	Tabasco sauce
1 cup	chopped scallions
1	red bell pepper, diced fine
1 lb.	fresh shrimp, peeled and diced
1 Tbsp.	salad oil
	Salt and pepper to taste

Mix all ingredients in large bowl. Heat griddle to 350°. Add 2 tablespoons oil to griddle. Spoon in 1 tablespoon of batter. Brown on both sides.

Yield: 15 appetizer servings.

Wasabi Fried Oysters with Lowcountry Pepper Sauce

12	extra select oysters
1/4 cup	wasabi paste
1/2 cup	Half & Half cream
1 cup	cornmeal breading
3 cups	frying oil

Marinate oysters in wasabi mixed with cream for 8 hours. Drain oysters and lightly coat with breading. Fry in 350° oil until golden brown. Serve over Lowcountry pepper sauce.

Lowcountry Pepper Sauce*

2	bell peppers
1 cup	cider vinegar
2 cups	water
3/4 cup	sugar
1 oz.	chopped garlic
1 oz.	granulated sugar
1 oz.	Tabasco sauce
1 oz.	tomato sauce
1 tsp.	salt

Seed and dice peppers. In a large saucepot, add all ingredients and bring to a boil, cooking for 10–20 minutes or until peppers are soft. Purée all ingredients in blender and return to saucepot. Thicken slightly with cornstarch. Let cool. Store at room temperature.

Yield: 2 appetizer servings.

* Leftover sauce will hold for two weeks in refrigerator

In the Pink

What puts the pink in flamingos? Shrimp of course. Flamingos turn pink from eating beta-carotene-rich shrimp, a dietary favorite of the birds. Flamingos that don't eat shrimp are white, of course. Shrimp is also America's favorite crustacean. While there are hundreds of shrimp species, most are classified as either warm-water shrimp or cold-water shrimp. As a general rule, the colder the water, the smaller and more succulent the shrimp.

82 Queen Deli Pickles

60	pickling cucumbers, quartered
15–20	cloves garlic
2	bunches fresh dill
½ cup	pickling spice
½ cup	dill seed
2 cups	sugar
1¼ cups	pickling salt
5 cups	white vinegar
10 qt.	water

Bring water, sugar, and salt to a boil; let cool to room temperature. Place cucumbers in jar with garlic, dill, and other spices. Pour pickling mixture over cucumbers; chill for 2 days. Keep refrigerated.

Yield: 60 pickles.

Black-Eyed Pea Relish

8 (16 oz.) cans	black-eyed peas, drained and rinsed
1	red bell pepper, diced fine
1	yellow bell pepper, diced fine
1	bunch scallions, chopped
½ cup	brown sugar
1 cup	cider vinegar
4 oz.	salad oil
1 Tbsp.	salt
1 Tbsp.	black pepper
1 Tbsp.	garlic, chopped
2 oz.	Jalapeño Tabasco sauce

In a medium mixing bowl, combine all ingredients and mix gently. This is best if made the day before using. Great on grilled fish, pork, or chicken. Can be stored in refrigerator for up to 30 days.

Yield: 1 gallon.

Caper Relish

 1 (32 oz.) jar capers
     1 red onion, diced fine
     1 large or 2 small red bell peppers, diced fine
     1 green bell pepper, diced fine

Mix all ingredients together. Great topping for grilled fish or chicken.

Yield: 1 quart.

Corn Relish

   5 lb. frozen kernel corn
    2 red bell peppers, diced fine
    2 green bell peppers, diced fine
  1/2 cup cider vinegar
  1/2 tsp. cayenne pepper
  2 Tbsp. brown sugar
    1 red onion, diced fine
  1/4 cup olive oil
   1 tsp. salt

Thaw corn and drain off all excess water. In mixing bowl, add all ingredients and mix well. Best served at room temperature.

Yield: 1 quart.

Cranberry Relish

  6 lbs. cranberries
 4 cups sugar
 2 cups vinegar
 4 cups water
  1 tsp. garlic, chopped
    6 cinnamon sticks

Combine all ingredients in a heavy sauce pot. Cook for 20 minutes, then chill.

Yield: 2 1/2 quarts.

Pineapple Relish

1	pineapple, skinned, cored, and diced
1	red bell pepper, diced fine and rinsed
1	fresh jalapeño pepper, diced fine
2 Tbsp.	sugar
1 Tbsp.	olive oil or salad oil
1/4 cup	apple cider vinegar
1 Tbsp.	mint, chopped
	Salt and pepper to taste

In medium-size bowl, add all ingredients and mix well. Best if made 6 hours before using so flavors have time to blend.

Yield: 12 servings.

Red Pepper Jelly

4	large red bell peppers, diced fine
1 qt.	water
2 cups	cider vinegar
1 oz.	Texas Pete hot sauce
2 cups	sugar
5	bay leaves
2	sticks cinnamon
1	lemon rind, grated
2 oz.	plain gelatin

Bring all ingredients except gelatin to a boil. Sprinkle gelatin over surface, stirring constantly. Refrigerate overnight.

Yield: 2 quarts.

Roasted Corn & Tomato Relish

5	ripe tomatoes, diced very fine
1 cup	corn, roasted
1/4	large white onion, diced very fine
2	green peppers, diced very fine
2	cinnamon sticks
1 Tbsp.	garlic
1/2 cup	vinegar
1 cup	sugar
1 tsp.	salt
1/4 box	cornstarch

Place corn on a baking pan and roast at 400° until it lightly browns, about 30 minutes, stirring occasionally. While corn is roasting, combine all other ingredients, except cornstarch, in a large saucepan and bring to a boil. Slowly stir in cornstarch dissolved in water and reduce to simmer. Add roasted corn and allow to simmer for 5 minutes.

Yield: 1 quart.

Tomato Jalapeño Salsa

15	tomatoes, seeded and peeled
1	red onion, diced
8	jalapeño peppers, seeded
1 oz.	garlic, chopped
1/2 bunch	parsley, rinsed and chopped fine
2 oz.	olive oil
4 oz.	cider vinegar
2 oz.	sugar
	Salt and white pepper to taste

Chop all ingredients, except parsley, in food processor (do not purée). Add chopped parsley and season. Serve at room temperature for best flavor.

Yield: 2 quarts.

Apple & Orange Chutney

10	oranges, peeled, seeded, and diced
8	apples, cored and diced with skin on
1/2 cup	lemon juice
1 cup	brown sugar
4	cinnamon sticks
1 Tbsp.	garlic, chopped fine
1 tsp.	salt
1/2 tsp.	white pepper

In heavy saucepan, combine all ingredients and simmer slowly for 1 hour. Remove from heat and chill overnight for maximum flavor.

Yield: 1 quart.

Apple-Mint Chutney

Great on pork, veal, or beef.

25	Granny Smith apples, diced
1	large onion
1 cup	fresh mint, chopped
1/2 cup	lemon juice, freshly squeezed
1/2 cup	apple cider vinegar
1 lb.	brown sugar
2 Tbsp.	garlic
1 Tbsp.	salt
5	cinnamon sticks
1 box	raisins
2 lb. jar	mint jelly

In a heavy-duty sauce pot, combine all ingredients and slowly cook for 30–40 minutes until all ingredients are soft and chutney is reduced to a thick consistency. Serve at room temperature. Can be stored in refrigerator for months.

Yield: 2 quarts.

Apple or Pear Chutney

20	pears or apples
1 lb.	box raisins
3 cups	water
3 cups	white sugar
4	cinnamon sticks
1 tsp.	ground cinnamon
1 Tbsp.	salt
2 cups	apple cider vinegar
1 Tbsp.	garlic, chopped

Peel and dice pears (or apples) to a medium size. Put all ingredients in heavy saucepan and slowly cook for 1 hour.

Yield: 2 quarts.

Cranberry & Gold Raisin Chutney

1 lb.	cranberries, washed
1 1/2 cups	sugar
1 cup	apple cider vinegar
1 cup	water
1/2 lb.	gold raisins
3 Tbsp.	fresh garlic, chopped
3	cinnamon sticks
1/2 tsp.	salt

Combine all ingredients in a heavy saucepan. Cook slowly for 20 minutes, then chill. Best if made day before it is to be used. Serve at room temperature.

Yield: 4 cups.

Fig Chutney

7 lbs.	figs
1	onion
4 cups	cider vinegar
4 cups	sugar
2 oz.	garlic, chopped
2 Tbsp.	ground cinnamon
5	cinnamon sticks
2 lbs.	raisins
2 Tbsp.	salt
1 Tbsp.	black pepper

Combine all ingredients. Bring to a boil, then reduce heat. Simmer for about one hour until desired thickness is reached. Stir to prevent scorching on bottom.

Yield: 2 quarts.

Kiwi Chutney

40	kiwis, peeled and diced fine
1	red onion, diced fine
2	large red bell peppers, diced fine
2	large green bell peppers, diced fine
2	large yellow bell peppers, diced fine
2 cups	cider vinegar
1 cup	sugar
5	cinnamon sticks
	Salt and white pepper to taste

Combine onions, peppers, vinegar, sugar, and cinnamon sticks in a sauce pan. Bring to a boil and thicken with cornstarch to the consistency of syrup. Allow mixture to cook and add to the diced kiwi. Season to taste.

Yield: 2 quarts.

Pineapple-Mango Chutney

1	ripe pineapple, peeled and diced into small pieces
3	ripe mangos, peeled, seeded, and diced
1 cup	apple cider vinegar
1 cup	white sugar
1 Tbsp.	cinnamon
1 Tbsp.	fresh garlic, chopped
1 tsp.	salt
1 tsp.	white pepper
1 cup	water

Combine all ingredients in heavy saucepan. Bring to a boil, then reduce heat and simmer for 20–30 minutes until fruit is soft and mixture has thickened slightly. Remove from heat and cool at room temperature for 1 hour. Refrigerate. Will last for 2 weeks in refrigerator.

Yield: 1 quart

Salads, Dressings & Vegetables

Lowcountry Cooking with 82 Queen

Salads

82 Queen Chicken Almond Salad ... 33
82 Queen Grilled Portobello Mushroom Salad ... 33
Asparagus & Wild Mushroom Salad ... 34
Chicken Cashew Salad ... 34
Chicken Pecan Salad ... 35
Grilled Chicken & Green Bean Salad ... 35
Pulled Chicken & Wild Rice Salad ... 36
Red Bliss Potato Salad ... 36
Shrimp & Cucumber Salad ... 37

Dressings

Apple Vinaigrette ... 38
Balsamic Vinaigrette ... 38
Basil Oil ... 39
Blood Orange Vinaigrette ... 39
Creamy Pepper Dressing ... 39
Creole Mustard Vinaigrette ... 40
Dijon Vinaigrette ... 40
Gorgonzola Dressing ... 41
Honey Lime & Mint Dressing ... 41
Poppy Seed & Balsamic Vinaigrette ... 41
Raspberry Vinaigrette ... 42
Sherry Mayonnaise ... 42

Vegetables

Creamed Spinach ... 43
Fried Green Tomatoes with Lowcountry Pepper Sauce ... 43
Lowcountry Collard Greens ... 44
Holiday Acorn Squash ... 45
Whipped Sweet Potatoes ... 45

616-A Wappoo Road • Charleston, SC 29407
843.556.3400

82 Queen Chicken Almond Salad

4	(8 oz.) chicken breasts, grilled
1	red bell pepper, chopped
1	gold bell pepper, chopped
½	red onion, chopped
2 oz.	grain Dijon mustard
1 tsp.	balsamic vinegar
½ cup	mayonnaise
¼ cup	almonds, slivered and toasted

Cut chicken breasts into ¼-inch cubes. Combine all other ingredients in mixing bowl and let stand 4–6 hours to increase flavor. Add salt and pepper to taste. Serve over crisp romaine lettuce with fresh fruit.

Yield: 4 servings.

82 Queen Grilled Portobello Mushroom Salad

4–6	Portobello mushrooms, 5-inch diameter, stems removed
2 cups	oil
2	sprigs rosemary
1 tsp.	salt
1 tsp.	black pepper
1 tsp.	garlic

Mix oil, rosemary, salt, pepper, and garlic. Place mushrooms in a shallow pie pan and pour marinade over; let marinate for 1–2 hours or overnight. Mushrooms will absorb most of the marinade. Grill mushrooms, 5–8 minutes per side, until tender. Remove, slice, and arrange mushrooms on a plate and top with balsamic vinaigrette. Garnish with goat cheese and serve on a bed of gourmet greens.

Vinaigrette

3 tsp.	balsamic vinegar
1 tsp.	olive oil
1 tsp.	brown sugar
Dash	salt and pepper

Combine all ingredients and mix well.

Yield: 6 servings.

Asparagus & Wild Mushroom Salad

2 lb.	fresh asparagus
1 cup	wild mushrooms (shiitake or oyster preferably)
1	large sweet red pepper
1	small red onion
1 cup	creamy pepper dressing

Clean asparagus and cut into 1-inch pieces. Poach in simmering water for 1 minute. Chill in ice bath. Drain well. Julienne pepper into 1-inch pieces. Dice red onion. Mix all ingredients together and let marinate for 1 hour.

Yield: 12 servings.

Chicken Cashew Salad

5 (7 oz.)	skinless chicken breasts, grilled, chilled, and cubed
½ stalk	celery bias-cut, thin
2	green bell peppers, diced large cubes
½ cup	green onions, chopped
½ cup	roasted cashews
	Dressing

Grill chicken, being careful not to overcook. Put all ingredients in large mixing bowl. Make dressing in separate bowl, then blend both together.

Dressing

1 cup	mayonnaise
3 oz.	Dijon mustard
1 oz.	lemon juice
1 oz.	Worcestershire sauce
1 Tbsp.	salt
½ Tbsp.	white pepper

Yield: 8 servings.

Chicken Pecan Salad

3–5 lb.	cooked chicken meat, diced small
1 stalk	celery, diced small
2 tsp.	onions, chopped fine
½ tsp.	dry mustard
1½ cups	mayonnaise
½ tsp.	black pepper
½ tsp.	Worcestershire
1 cup	pecan pieces
	Salt to taste

Chill meat only. Combine all ingredients in a large bowl.

Yield: 15 servings.

Grilled Chicken & Green Bean Salad

5 (7 oz.)	chicken breasts
1	red bell pepper, julienne
1	green bell pepper, julienne
1	small red onion, julienne
½ lb.	green beans (fresh)
	Dressing

Grill chicken, being careful not to overcook. Let chill and cut into ¼-inch strips. Julienne peppers and onions ¼-inch wide. Place in large mixing bowl. Poach green beans until half tender. Chill in ice bath. Drain well and place in bowl. Mix dressing in a separate bowl and add to salad. Mix well and serve chilled with fresh fruit.

Dressing

1 cup	mayonnaise
6 oz.	Creole mustard
1 tsp.	cider vinegar
1 tsp.	sugar
	Salt and white pepper to taste

Yield: 6–8 servings.

Pulled Chicken & Wild Rice Salad

1	whole chicken, cut into fourths
1 cup	wild rice mix (Uncle Ben's)
2 cups	celery, julienned
1/2 cup	onion, diced
1 cup	fresh mushrooms, sliced
1 cup	red bell pepper, diced medium
1/2 cup	salad oil
1/4 cup	brown sugar
1/4 cup	apple cider vinegar
2 Tbsp.	fresh cut tarragon
2 tsp.	salt
1 tsp.	cracked black pepper
2 Tbsp.	Dijon mustard

Poach or steam chicken for 30 minutes until meat falls off the bone; chill and pull meat from bone. Discard skin and bone; cut meat into small bite-size pieces. Cook wild rice mix as per package instructions. Place on sheet pan and refrigerate until cool. In large mixing bowl, place chicken, wild rice, and all remaining ingredients. Toss gently.

Yield: 8 servings.

Red Bliss Potato Salad

5 lb.	red bliss potatoes, cut into small wedges
2 cups	celery, diced medium
1 cup	green onion, diced
1	red bell pepper, diced fine
1/4 cup	fresh dill, chopped
	Dressing

Steam or boil potatoes until just tender and let cool. Add dressing and remaining ingredients. Toss gently.

Dressing

1 cup	sour cream
2 cups	mayonnaise
1 Tbsp.	salt
1 tsp.	white pepper
1 Tbsp.	dry mustard
1/2 cup	Parmesan cheese, grated

In mixing bowl, add all ingredients and mix well.

Yield: 1–20 side dish servings.

Shrimp & Cucumber Salad

1 lb.	medium shrimp, peeled, boiled, drained, and cooled
1	medium onion, diced
1	green bell pepper. diced
1/2 cup	celery, diced
2	cucumbers, peeled, seeded, and diced
1 cup	mayonnaise
2 Tbsp.	fresh dill, chopped
2 Tbsp.	lemon juice
2	dashes Tabasco sauce
	Salt and pepper to taste

Combine all ingredients in large mixing bowl. Add salt and pepper to taste.

Yield: 4–6 servings.

Apple Vinaigrette

2	egg yolks
1 tsp.	Dijon mustard
¼ cup	apple cider vinegar
1½ cups	salad oil
2 Tbsp.	sugar
1	shallot, diced fine
1	Granny Smith apple, peeled, cored, and finely diced
	Salt and pepper to taste

Mix egg yolks and mustard. Slowly add oil while whipping constantly. Blend in vinegar and add remaining ingredients. This is best if made a day before needed.

Yield: 2 cups.

Balsamic Vinaigrette

6	egg yolks
8 oz.	balsamic vinegar
3 cups	olive oil
1	red onion, diced fine
1	red pepper, diced fine
3	green bell peppers, diced fine
½ cup	sugar
	Salt and white pepper to taste
2 oz.	Dijon mustard

Blend egg yolks, balsamic vinegar, and Dijon mustard in a large mixer. While blending, slowly pour in olive oil. Add remaining ingredients and season.

Yield: 1 quart.

Basil Oil

1	bunch fresh basil
1/2	bulb garlic
1 tsp.	salt
1/2 tsp.	black pepper

Stuff basil, garlic, salt, and pepper into a glass bottle. Pour hot olive oil into bottle. Let cool, then seal top. Best if used after 48 hours so flavor has time to peak.

Yield: 1 quart.

Blood Orange Vinaigrette

3 cups	Canola Oil
1 cup	Rice Wine Vinegar
3	Blood Oranges (juiced)
1/2 cup	sugar
	Salt and Pepper to taste

Blend all ingredients in food processor, except oil. Slowly add oil to ingredients until emulsified.

Yield: 4 cups.

Creamy Pepper Dressing

1 cup	mayonnaise
1/2 cup	milk
1 Tbsp.	black pepper
1 Tbsp.	Parmesan cheese
1 Tbsp.	onion, chopped
1 tsp.	lemon juice
1 tsp.	cider vinegar
1 tsp.	Worcestershire Sauce
1 tsp.	garlic, chopped
1/4 tsp.	Tabasco sauce

Mix all ingredients together well.

Yield: 2 cups.

Creole Mustard Vinaigrette

- 2 oz. Dijon mustard
- 2 oz. Creole grain mustard (found in gourmet section)
- 1 cup apple cider vinegar
- 3 cups vegetable oil
- 2 tsp. salt
- 1 tsp. white pepper
- 1/2 cup light brown sugar

In large mixing bowl, combine the Dijon mustard, Creole mustard, and half of the vinegar. Using a hand mixer or electric whisk, blend ingredients for 30 seconds, then slowly add vegetable oil while constantly mixing. After all the oil has been blended in, slowly add remaining half-cup of vinegar, salt, pepper, and sugar.

Yield: 1 quart.

Dijon Vinaigrette

- 3 cups oil
- 1 cup vinegar
- 8 oz. grain Dijon mustard
- 1/4 cup sugar
- 1 tsp. black pepper
- 1 tsp. salt
- 1/2 cup onion, chopped fine
- 2 bay leaves
- 1 tsp. thyme
- 1 tsp. garlic, chopped
- 1 egg yolk

Combine egg yolk and mustard in a medium-size bowl. Using a whisk, slowly blend in the oil. Mixture should be slightly thick. Add all other ingredients and blend well. Chill 24 hours.

Yield: 1 quart.

Gorgonzola Dressing

   1 qt. mayonnaise
   1/2 lb. Gorgonzola cheese, crumbled
   1 oz. Worcestershire sauce
   1/2 tsp. white pepper
   1 Tbsp. lemon juice
   1 tsp. salt
   1 cup cold water

Mix all ingredients together. Keep chilled.

               Yield: 1 1/2 quarts.

Honey Lime & Mint Dressing

   1 qt. heavy cream
   1/4 cup honey
   1/2 cup sugar
   1/2 cup lime juice (fresh squeezed)
   1/8 cup fresh mint leaves, chopped

Using chilled stainless steel bowl, whisk cream until thick (should form peaks). Gently fold in sugar, honey, lime juice, and mint. Keep chilled. Use quickly.

               Yield: 1 1/4 quart.

Poppy Seed & Balsamic Vinaigrette

   2 egg yolks
   4 oz. balsamic vinegar
   8 oz. olive oil
   1/2 red onion, diced fine
   1/2 red bell pepper, diced fine
   1/2 green bell pepper, diced fine
   2 Tbsp. sugar
    Salt and white pepper to taste

Blend egg yolks and balsamic vinegar in stainless steel bowl. While whisking mixture, slowly pour in olive oil. Add remaining ingredients and season to taste.

               Yield: 3/4 pint.

Raspberry Vinaigrette

- 2 oz. raspberry sauce or melba sauce
- 2 oz. cider vinegar
- 1 cup salad oil
- 1 tsp. sugar
- 1 pinch of white pepper

In a large stainless steel bowl, blend all ingredients together except oil. Slowly whisk oil into mixture until completely blended.

Yield: 1 pint.

Sherry Mayonnaise

- 2 cups salad oil
- 3 egg yolks
- 1/8 cup lemon juice
- 1/8 cup sherry
- 1 Tbsp. cider vinegar
- 1/2 tsp. Dijon mustard
- 1/2 tsp. salt
- 1/4 tsp. white pepper
- 1/4 tsp. sugar

Put all ingredients in a mixing bowl except for the salad oil and sherry. Mix with an electric mixer for 1 minute, slowly adding oil. Mayonnaise will thicken and take on a white color. When mixture is finished, whisk in sherry.

Yield: 2 1/2 cups.

CREAMED SPINACH

1 1/2 lb.	spinach, washed
2 Tbsp.	butter
2 Tbsp.	flour
2 cups	heavy cream
4 oz.	chicken boullion
1	yellow onion, julienned
1 oz.	garlic, chopped
	Salt and white pepper to taste

In a saucepan, melt butter over low heat. Add flour and whisk until it makes a pasty roux. Add liquid and bring to boil. Add remaining ingredients.

Yield: 6–8 servings.

FRIED GREEN TOMATOES WITH LOWCOUNTRY PEPPER SAUCE

2	large green tomatoes
1 cup	all-purpose flour
2 cups	corn meal
1 tsp.	chopped parsley
1 tsp.	salt
1/2 tsp.	white pepper
3	eggs
1 cup	milk
1 qt.	peanut oil or canola oil

Prepare a breading station using three bowls: one for flour, one for egg wash (mix milk and eggs), and one for breading mixture (salt, pepper and corn meal). Slice tomatoes 1/4-inch thick. Place tomatoes in flour, then egg wash, then breading mixture. Let breaded tomato slices rest 10 minutes on waxed paper. Fry in 350° oil until golden brown.

Lowcountry Pepper Sauce

8	red bell peppers, seeded and diced
1 qt.	cider vinegar
2 qt.	water
3 cups	sugar
2 oz.	garlic, chopped
2 oz.	granulated sugar
4 oz.	Tabasco sauce
4 oz.	tomato paste
2 Tbsp.	salt

Place all ingredients in a large saucepot. Bring to a boil for 10–20 minutes until peppers are soft. Puree all ingredients in large blender. Return sauce to pot. Thicken slightly with cornstarch. Will keep in refrigerator up to 2 months.

Yield: 1 gallon.

Fresh is Best

According to 82 Queen Chef Proprietor Steve Kish, one of the reasons the food is so good in Charleston is because so much of it is grown locally. "instead of two or three days on a truck, we get our produce from Johns Island fresh-picked," says Kish. Asparagus, broccoli, brussels sprouts, collards, corn, cucumbers, eggplant, lettuce, okra, onions, peppers, spinach, tomatoes, yellow squash, and zucchini head the list of vegetables grown here. Throw a few locally grown herbs in the soup pot to spice things up. And with its extra-long growing season, the Charleston area has an almost inexhaustible supply of "fresh" almost year-round. Did you know that Johns Island operates the largest tomato packing facility in the country? South Carolina tomatoes now reach dining tables throughout the eastern United States.

Lowcountry Collard Greens

12	slices bacon
1	sweet onion, julienned
1	bunch collard greens, washed thoroughly and chopped
2 Tbsp.	Tabasco sauce
2 oz.	vinegar
1/3 cup	sugar
1 tsp.	black pepper
	Salt to taste

Dice bacon and brown in pot. Add julienned onion and sauté in bacon grease until tender. Add greens and cover with water. Add remaining ingredients and simmer until tender. Adjust seasoning to taste.

Yield: 12 servings.

Holiday Acorn Squash

3	acorn squash
1	orange or tangerine
½ cup	raisins
½ cup	brown sugar
1 tsp.	cinnamon or nutmeg
	Salt and white pepper to taste

Cut a 1-inch slice out of the middle of each squash and set aside, leaving the ends to form cups. Cut a small piece off of the bottom of each squash cup to allow them to stand up. Clean the seeds out and hollow all but ½ inch around the skin. Peel the set-aside slice and dice the remaining squash. Blanch the diced squash and the squash cups in simmering water until they are almost tender. Cool immediately. Peel orange, reserving the skin. Seed and dice orange sections. Zest half of the orange peel. Toss with the raisins, ¼ cup brown sugar, cinnamon or nutmeg, salt, and white pepper. Fill cups with mixture and top with remaining brown sugar. Bake at 350° for 20 to 25 minutes.

Yield: 6 servings.

Whipped Sweet Potatoes

4	large sweet potatoes, skinned and steamed until very soft
1 pt.	heavy cream
1 tsp.	ground cinnamon
½ cup	brown sugar
	Salt and white pepper to taste

Add all ingredients to potatoes and beat together. Keep hot until served.

Yield: 8–10 servings.

Eat your Veggies

Do you struggle to get your kids to eat their vegetables? Maybe you're not serving the right one. Try plunking down a ripe juicy South Carolina watermelon and watch their happy faces light up. This sweet treat is actually a vegetable masquerading as a fruit. Cousin to the cucumber and kin to the gourd, watermelons range in size from seven to over 100 pounds. By the way, the tomato is a fruit masquerading as a vegetable.

Photo: Chris Cassidy

GRITS, RICE, PASTA & BREAD

Lowcountry Cooking with 82 Queen

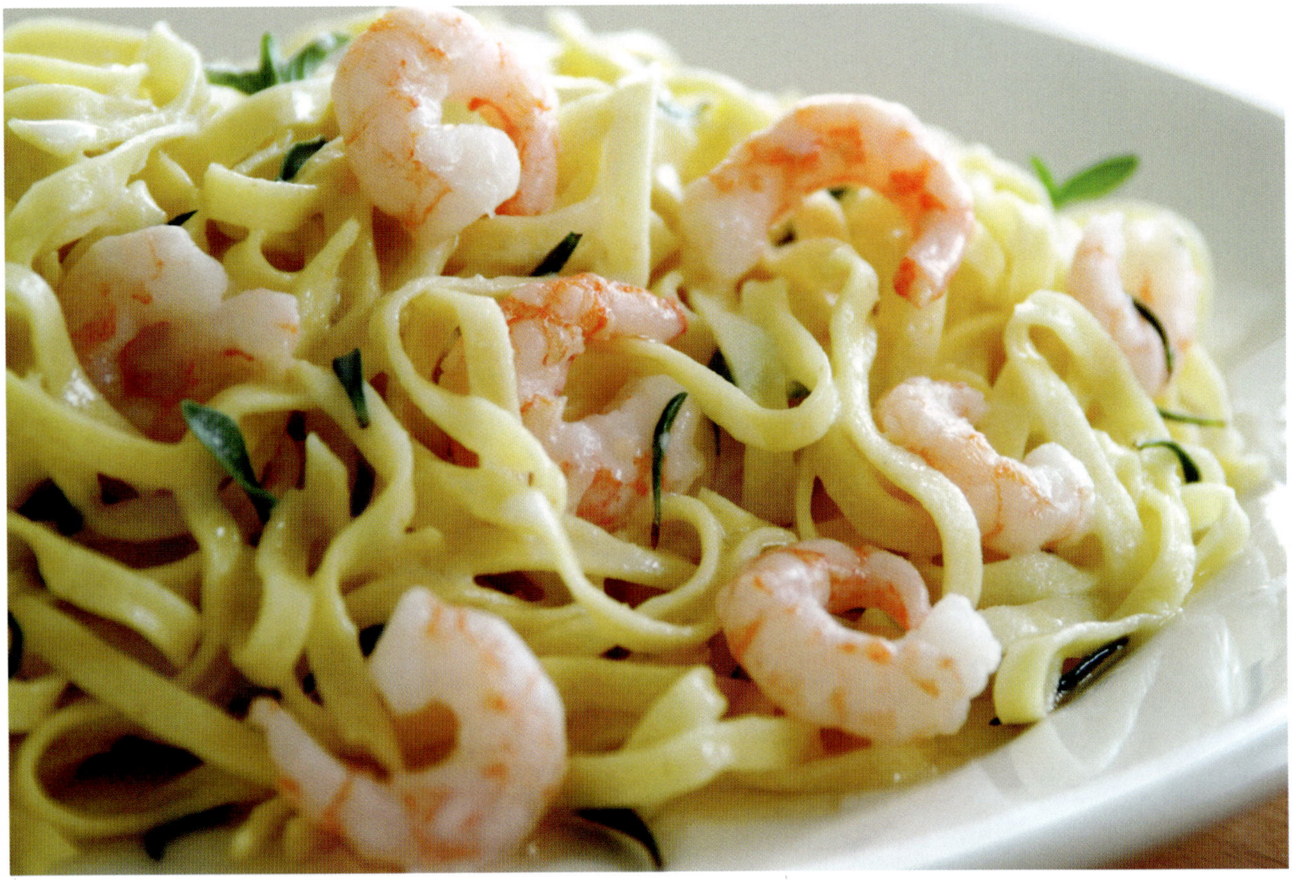

Grits

82 Queen World Famous BBQ Shrimp & Grits ... 50

Grits ... 51

Grits Cakes ... 51

Grilled Salmon & Grits ... 52

Rice

Crawfish or Shrimp Étouffée ... 53

Tasso Chicken & Shrimp ... 54

Pasta

Basil Linguine with Crawfish ... 55

Pasta and Prosciutto Ham ... 56

Pasta with Sautéed Shrimp & Scallops in Creamed Spinach and Tomato ... 57

Pesto Linguine with Tomatoes & Balsamic Vinegar ... 58

Shrimp & Orzo Salad ... 58

Bread

Corn Muffins ... 59

Dill Bread ... 59

Fruit Bread ... 60

Harvest Cornbread ... 60

Holiday Cranberry Bread ... 61

82 Queen World Famous BBQ Shrimp & Grits

2 lb.	shrimp
1 Tbsp.	butter
	Southern Comfort BBQ Sauce
	Lowcountry Grits

Sauté shrimp in butter or poach in lightly salted water for 1 minute. Serve over Lowcountry grits. Garnish with bacon crumbles, scallions and grated cheddar cheese.

BBQ Sauce

1/4 lb.	bacon, diced
1/2 cup	red onion, diced fine
1/2 cup	red bell pepper
1/2 cup	green bell pepper
2 (14 oz.)	bottles Heinz ketchup
1/2 cup	brown sugar
3–4 Tbsp.	bourbon liquor
	Salt and pepper to taste

Cook bacon until half-done. Add onions and peppers; sauté until done. Add bourbon. Carefully light so that it flames and burns off alcohol. When flames disappear, add remaining ingredients and season to taste. Simmer for 10 minutes then cool. Will last under refrigeration for several weeks.

Lowcountry Grits

3 cups	heavy cream
1/4 lb.	butter
3 cups	water
1 cup	quick grits
	Salt and white pepper to taste

Heat cream and water to boil. Add butter, salt and pepper. Slowly add grits and reduce heat. Cook 20 minutes, being careful not to scorch mixture.

Yield: 6 dinner servings.

Grits

1½ cups quick grits
½ lb. butter
1 qt. heavy cream
1 qt. water
Salt and white pepper to taste

Bring water, cream, and butter to a simmer. Add grits, salt, and pepper and simmer very slowly for about 20 minutes.

Yield: 12 servings.

Grits Cakes

Warm grits
Bacon diced and cooked
Parsley, chopped
Flour
Egg wash
Bread crumbs

Great way to use up leftover grits. Add cooked, diced bacon and chopped parsley to warm, leftover grits. Pour onto greased cookie sheet pan and chill. Cut into 2 x 2-inch squares. Bread the squares using the 3-stage method of flour, egg wash, and bread crumbs. Cakes can be deep-fried or pan-fried. Great side for brunch or dinner.

Yield: dependent on leftover grits.

Royal Title

The World Grits Festival is held every April in St. George, S.C. Located about 60 miles northwest of Charleston, the town claims the title of "Grits Capital of the World." Its townsfolk reportedly eat more grits per person than any other place in the world.

Grilled Salmon & Grits

6 (7–8 oz.)	salmon fillets
1	medium red onion, julienned
3 Tbsp.	crumbled bacon
2 Tbsp.	capers
2 Tbsp.	butter
2 oz.	chardonnay wine
	Grits

Rub salmon with olive oil. Season with salt and pepper. Cook on a hot grill for 3–4 minutes per side. Salmon should be slightly translucent and pink in the middle. While salmon is cooking, sauté red onions in butter until soft. Add bacon and capers and cook 1 more minute. Deglaze with chardonnay. Serve salmon over grits and top with sautéed onion mixture.

Grits

1/2 lb.	butter
1 qt.	heavy cream
1 qt.	water
	Salt to taste
	White pepper to taste
1 1/2 cups	quick grits

Bring liquid ingredients to a simmer, then add remaining ingredients.

Yield: 12 servings.

True Grits

First made by Native Americans, grits are small broken grains of corn. True Southerners agree that grits are a dietary staple and dining tradition. But trying to get any two Southerners to agree on the best way to prepare them is nearly impossible. Shrimp, cream, cheese, eggs, Tasso ham, sausage, and even bacon grease can make their way into one of the many dishes featuring grits. Over 15 years ago, 82 Queen added an unusual zing to grits when it introduced barbequed shrimp and grits to its menu. A favorite of locals and visitors alike, this house specialty holds a permanent spot on the restaurant's menu.

Crawfish or Shrimp Étouffée

2 lb.	crawfish or shrimp
½ cup	onion, sliced
½ cup	cooked bacon
1 cup	celery, sliced
2 cups	Cajun red sauce

Combine washed crawfish or shrimp and Cajun red sauce; let simmer 4 minutes before adding other ingredients. Let simmer 7–10 minutes. Serve hot over fluffy white rice.

Cajun Red Sauce

¼ lb.	butter
¼ cup	flour
¼ cup	fresh lemon juice
¼ cup	Worcestershire sauce
2 Tbsp.	thyme
1 Tbsp.	garlic, chopped
1 tsp.	salt
	Bacon fat and drippings
8 oz.	white wine
1 (32 oz.)	can V-8 juice
1 tsp.	cayenne pepper
¼ cup	brown sugar
4	bay leaves
1 tsp.	black pepper

In a large, heavy saucepan, melt butter over low heat. Add flour and whisk until it makes a pasty roux. Add V-8 juice and all other ingredients.

Yield: 6 servings.

The Origin of BBQ

What's the origin of the word "barbecue"? It was the first used by French-speaking pirates who referred to a Caribbean pork feast as, "de barbe et queue," which translates, "from beard to tail." The pirates observed that the hog was an eminently versatile animal that could be consumed from head to toe. Today, barbecue has come to mean a method of slowly cooking meat, poultry, fish, or other food in a pit or a spit using hot coals or hardwood to generate the heat. The food is basted with a highly seasoned barbecue sauce to keep it moist. South Carolina and Texas boast the two most famous American regional barbecue styles.

Tasso Chicken & Shrimp

4 (8 oz.)	boneless chicken breasts
1/2 lb.	shrimp, peeled
1/4 lb.	Tasso ham, diced fine
1	onion, diced fine
1 Tbsp.	garlic, chopped
2 oz.	butter
2 Tbsp.	flour
1 pt.	Half & Half cream
1 cup	white rice
	Salt and pepper to taste

Grill chicken breasts. In large sauté pan, melt butter. Sauté tasso, onion, and garlic until onion is translucent. Dust with flour to absorb butter. Add Half & Half cream and bring to a boil, stirring constantly to prevent scorching. Add shrimp and reduce to a simmer. Let cook down to desired thickness. Season. Serve chicken breasts over rice, topped with shrimp and gravy mixture.

Yield: 4 servings.

In the early 1700s, planter near the coastal port of Charleston began the arduous process of clearing and dining inland swamps to provide water for the cultivation of rice. But the first attempts at growing it failed. Finally, in 1726, rice was successfully introduced into the colony, and with its success came the first wave of economic prosperity. In its rice heyday, Charleston Harbor was one of the largest shippers of rice in the world, second only to Bangkok. With the abolition of slavery, labor-intensive rice production screeched to a halt by the turn of the century. After a nearly hundred-year absence, rice is making a comeback in South Carolina. With the help of modern technology, Plumfield Plantation, located on the Great Pee Dee River near Darlington, reintroduced aromatic rice to South Carolina in 1996. The only colonial plantation to still offer rice commercially in the Carolinas, Plumfield Plantation proudly serves the truly distinctive taste of the 18th century Southern rice plantations.

Basil Linguine with Crawfish

1	small yellow onion, julienned
2 tsp.	fresh basil
1 lb.	crawfish tail meat
3 cups	basil linguine, cooked

Sauté onion and basil in olive oil. Add crawfish tail meat and cooked basil linguine, tossing until hot. Put into serving bowl and top with freshly grated Parmesan cheese.

Yield: 4–6 servings.

Pasta and Prosciutto Ham

1 1/2 cups	cooked pasta
4 oz.	prosciutto ham, sliced thin and cut into strips
	Fresh crabmeat to taste
1	red bell pepper, sliced
1 doz.	mushrooms
1 doz.	black olives
	Sherry, fresh basil (chopped), salt, and white wine to taste

Sauté peppers and mushrooms in butter. Add remaining ingredients and season with sherry, white wine, basil and salt. Serve hot with grated cheese.

Yield: 2 servings.

Pasta with Sautéed Shrimp & Scallops in Creamed Spinach and Tomato

3 doz.	shrimp, peeled
3 doz.	scallops
8 oz.	margarine
8 oz.	flour
½ gal.	milk
1 qt.	heavy cream
1 cup	diced tomatoes
1 cup	white wine
1	onion, diced fine
2 cups	chopped spinach
1 Tbsp.	chopped garlic
	Salt and white pepper to taste
	Fresh pasta

In a saucepan, melt margarine over low heat. Add flour and whisk until it makes a pasty roux. Add milk, cream, seafood base, wine, onions, spinach, garlic, and tomatoes, and bring to a boil, stirring constantly. Season, and simmer for an additional 5 minutes. Lightly sauté shrimp and scallops in ½-cup butter and ¼-cup wine and add to sauce. Serve over fresh pasta and garnish with shredded Parmesan cheese.

Yield: 6–8 servings.

Pesto Linguine with Tomatoes & Balsamic Vinegar

    5 oz.   peeled pear tomatoes
    2 oz.   Spanish onion
   1 Tbsp. fresh basil
   1 Tbsp. garlic
    2 oz.   extra virgin olive oil
    5 oz.   balsamic vinegar
    1 oz.   Parmesan cheese
            Salt and black pepper to taste
    3 oz.   pesto linguine

Heat the olive oil and garlic in a medium saucepan. Roughly chop the onion and tomatoes and add them to the saucepan. Cook over medium-high heat for 5–7 minutes. Cook the linguine "al dente," drain, and toss with the tomato sauce. Season with fresh basil, salt, and pepper. Just before serving, drizzle pasta with a quality aged balsamic vinegar and top with Parmesan shavings.

Yield: 1 serving.

Shrimp & Orzo Salad

    1 lb.   medium shrimp, steamed, peeled, drained
   1 cup celery, diced medium
      6   hard cooked eggs, diced
      1   small red onion, diced medium
      1   green bell pepper, diced medium
   3 cups cooked orzo
          Dressing

Poach shrimp and drain well in large bowl. Place shrimp, cut vegetables, and eggs in a separate bowl. Make dressing and combine both together and toss.

Dressing

   1 cup mayonnaise
   1 oz.   lemon juice
   2 oz.   fresh dill
   1 tsp. salt
  1/2 tsp. white pepper
  1/2 oz. dry mustard
  1 dash Tabasco sauce

Yield: 5–7 servings.

Corn Muffins

1 lb.	sugar
1/2 oz.	salt
1 1/2 pt.	milk
1 lb. 8 oz.	pastry flour
1 cup	mayonnaise
8 oz.	shortening
8	eggs
1 lb.	cornmeal
1 1/2 oz.	baking powder
1 cup	scallions, chopped

Cream sugar, shortening, and salt. Beat in eggs and stir in milk. Add cornmeal. Sift flour and baking powder and mix until smooth. Add mayonnaise and scallions. Bake for 20 minutes at 425°.

Yield: 4 dozen muffins.

Dill Bread

2 1/3 cups	flour
1	egg
1 Tbsp.	butter or margarine
2 Tbsp.	dill seed
1/4 tsp.	baking soda
1/4 cup	lukewarm water
1 cup	cottage cheese
2 Tbsp.	sugar
1 Tbsp.	onion, chopped
1 tsp.	salt
1 pkg.	yeast

Soften yeast with water and let stand for 10 minutes. In a large mixing bowl, combine the cheese, butter, sugar, salt, and baking soda. Add onion, dill seed, and yeast mixture. Cover and let rise until double in size. Knead and let rise for another 45 minutes. Bake at 350° for 30 minutes or until a toothpick inserted in the middle comes out clean. After you take the bread out, rub the top with butter and sprinkle with salt.

Yield: 1 loaf.

Fruit Bread

8	eggs
1 1/3 cups	shortening
2 2/3 cups	sugar
4 cups	flour
2 tsp.	salt
1 Tbsp. plus 1 tsp.	baking powder
4 cups	fruit
1 Tbsp.	syrup or vanilla

Cream eggs, shortening, and sugar. Add the remaining ingredients and mix well. Bake at 300° for 50 minutes. Allow to cool before wrapping. This recipe can be made with basically any cut fruit, such as apples, pears, peaches, strawberries, blackberries, orange, etc.

Yield: 2 loaves.

Harvest Cornbread

1 cup	flour
1/2 tsp.	salt
2 Tbsp.	sugar
1 cup	milk
1/3 cup	margarine or oil
1/3 cup	green bell pepper, chopped
2 tsp.	baking soda
1 cup	yellow cornmeal
1	egg
1 cup	tomatoes, chopped
1/2 cup	Cheddar cheese

Combine all ingredients and bake in a greased 8 x 8 x 2-inch baking pan. Bake in a preheated 400° oven for 25 minutes.

Yield: 1 loaf.

Holiday Cranberry Bread

2 cups	unbleached, all-purpose flour
1/2 cup	sugar
1 Tbsp.	baking powder
1/2 tsp.	salt
2/3 cup	fresh orange juice
2	eggs
3 Tbsp.	butter
1/2 cup	shelled walnuts, coarsely chopped
1 1/4 cups	cranberries (fresh)
2 tsp.	grated orange rind

Preheat oven to 350°. Grease an 8 x 4 x 3-inch bread pan. Sift flour, sugar, baking powder and salt into a mixing bowl. Make a well in the middle of the sifted mixture and pour in orange juice, eggs, and melted butter. Fold in walnuts, cranberries, and orange rind. Pour batter into the prepared pan and set on the middle rack of the oven. Bake for 45–50 minutes or until a knife inserted in the center comes out clean. Remove bread from the oven and cool in the pan for 10 minutes. After 10 minutes, remove bread from pan and allow to cool completely on rack. Wrap and put away for 1–2 days before serving.

Yield: 1 loaf.

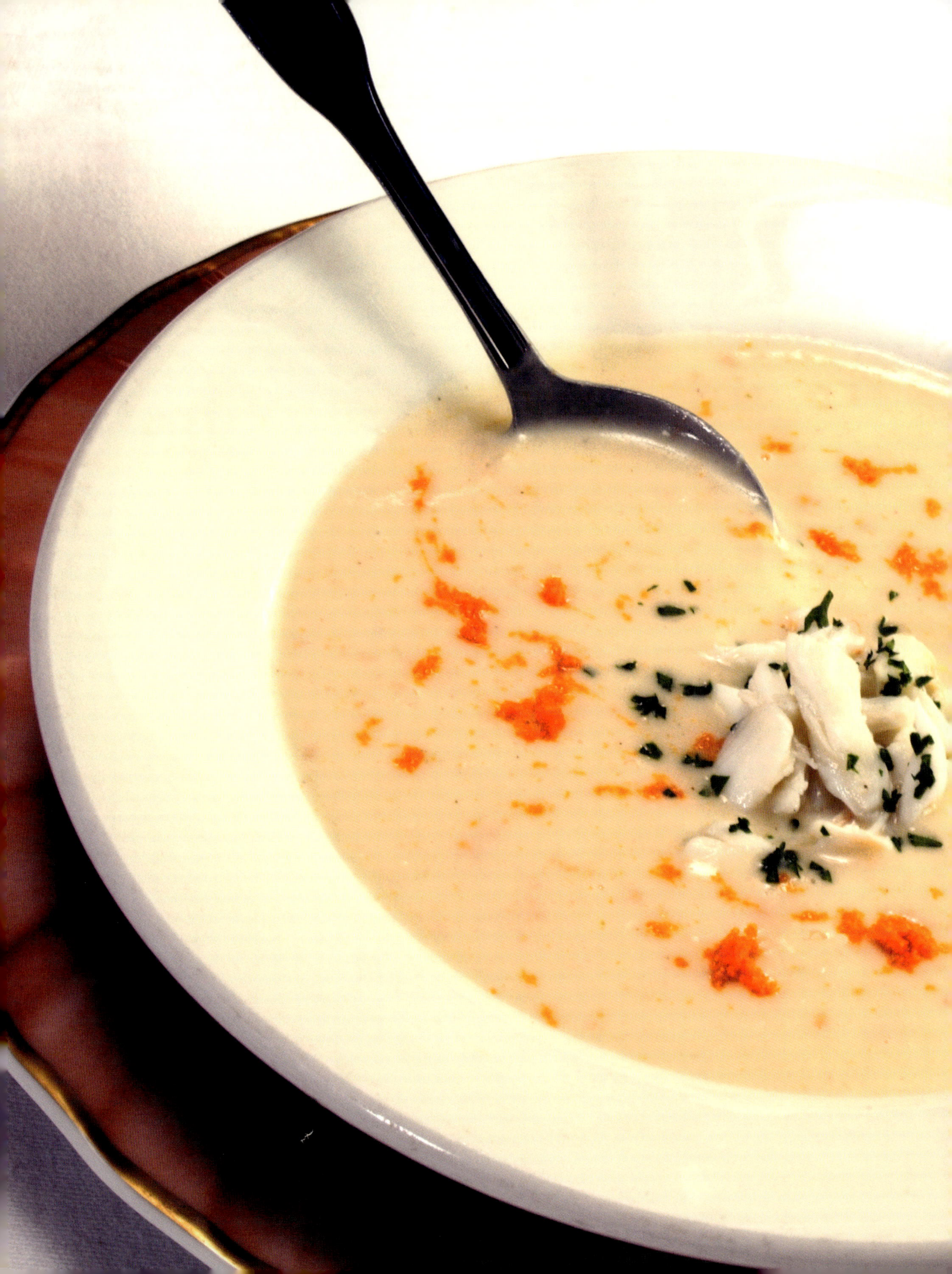

SOUPS, STOCKS & SAUCES

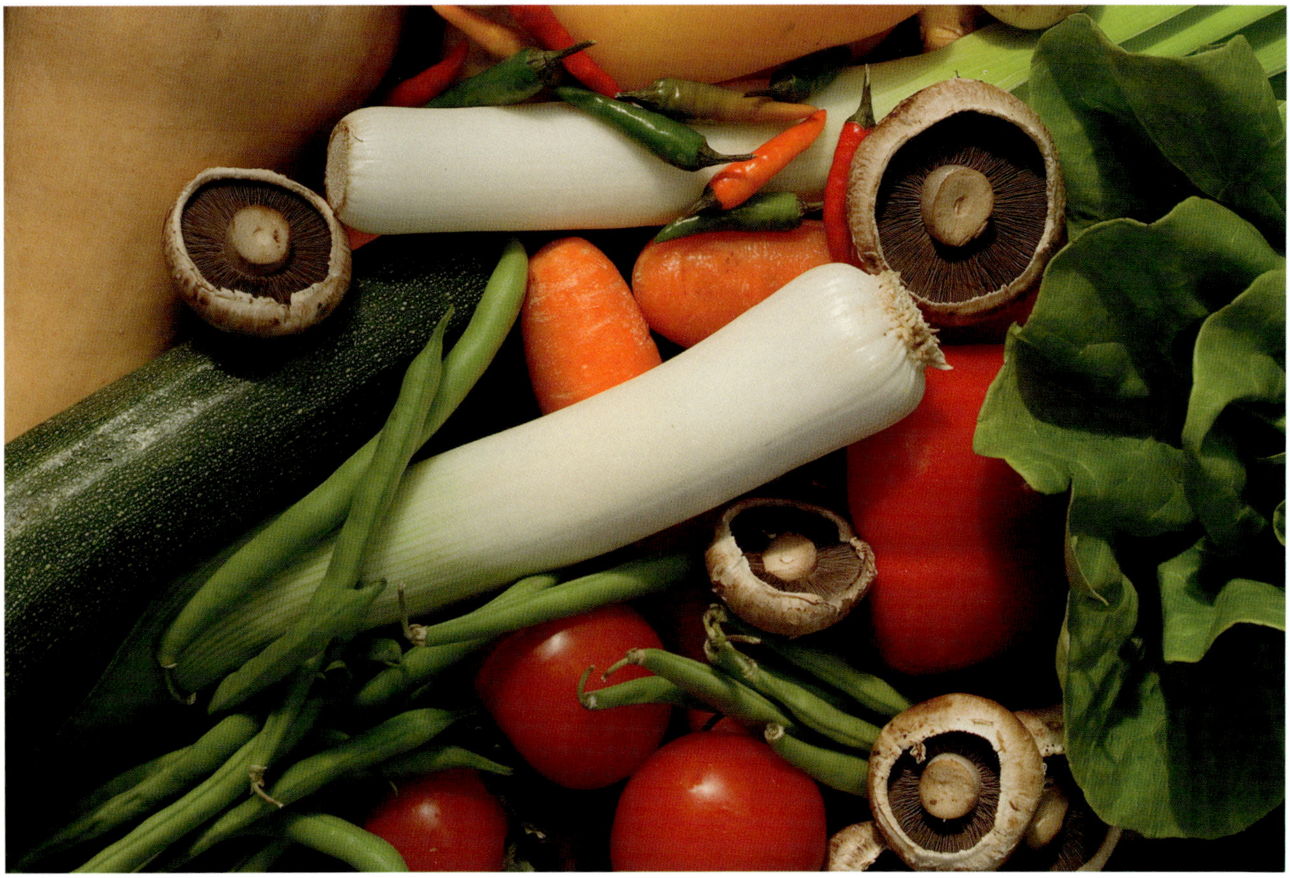

Soup

82 Queen Award-Winning She-Crab Soup ... 66
Black Bean Soup ... 67
Charleston Bean Soup ... 67
Corn & Vidalia Chowder ... 68
Crawfish Chowder ... 68
Oyster Chowder ... 69
Quail Consommé ... 70
Seafood Chowder ... 71
Shrimp Gazpacho ... 71
Wild Mushroom & Rice Soup ... 72
Wisconsin Cheddar Cheese Soup ... 72

Stock

Brown Stock ... 73
Chicken Stock ... 73
Fish Stock ... 74
Tomato Stock ... 74

Sauces

82 Queen Hollandaise ... 75
Basil Cream Sauce ... 76
Basil Tartar Sauce ... 76
Black Bean Sauce ... 77
Bourbon Cream ... 77
Charleston Spiced Mayonnaise ... 78
Cherry Grand Marnier Glaze ... 78
Chili Hollandaise ... 79
Cocktail Sauce ... 79
Cranberry & Apricot Glaze ... 80
Field Pea Sauce ... 80
Herb Seasoning Blend ... 81
Honey & Ginger Dipping Sauce ... 81
Jalapeño Sauce ... 81
Jambalaya Sauce ... 82
Orange Pepper Marmalade ... 82
Pesto ... 83
Praline Bourbon Glaze ... 83
Raspberry Orange Sauce ... 84
Red Pepper Sauce ... 84
Sweet Red Pepper Coulis ... 85
Soy Dipping Sauce ... 85
Tasso Gravy ... 85

82 Queen Award-Winning She-Crab Soup

1/4 lb.	butter
1/4 lb.	flour
3 cups	milk
1 cup	heavy cream
2 cups	fish stock or water and fish base
1 lb.	white crabmeat (special)
1/4 lb.	crab roe
1/4 cup	chopped carrots
1/4 cup	chopped onion
1 cup	chopped celery
1 Tbsp.	Tabasco sauce
1 Tbsp.	Worcestershire sauce

In a saucepan, melt butter over low heat. Add flour and whisk until it makes a pasty roux. Add milk and cream; bring to boil. Add lightly sautéed carrots, celery, and onion, and remaining ingredients; simmer for 20 minutes.

Yield: 12 servings.

Meet the Real Rhett Butler

Most everyone is familiar with Rhett Butler, the dashing southern gentleman of "Gone with the Wind" fame. But have you ever heard of William Deas? An African-American, Deas created she-crab soup, a Charleston specialty featuring crabmeat and crab roe in a creamy base. Deas first whipped up the now-famous concoction while he was the butler for Robert Goodwin Rhett, a former mayor of Charleston. William Deas was "Rhett's butler."

Black Bean Soup

1 lb.	black beans
1 gal.	water
½ lb.	smoked sausage, chopped
1	small onion, diced fine
1 tsp.	garlic, diced fine
4	pieces celery, diced fine
1	small carrot, diced fine
2 tsp.	salt
1 tsp.	black pepper
1 tsp.	chili powder
½ tsp.	cumin
4	dashes of Tabasco sauce

Soak beans overnight in cold water. Drain the beans the next day and add remaining ingredients. Bring to a boil. Boil for ½ hour, then reduce heat to medium. Cover and let cook for 2 hours, stirring frequently. Garnish with shredded Cheddar cheese, diced red onion, sour cream, and a slice of jalapeño pepper.

Yield: 15 servings.

Charleston Bean Soup

1 gal.	water
1 lb.	3-bean mix
2 oz.	ham base or ham hocks (if available)
1	celery stalk, chopped fine
1	onion, chopped fine
1	carrot, chopped fine
2 oz.	cider vinegar
1 tsp.	garlic, chopped
1 tsp.	Tabasco sauce
3	bay leaves
	Salt and pepper to taste

Cook all ingredients until beans are broken up and soup acquires a thickness. If water evaporates, more may be added to prevent scorching. Garnish soup with roasted country ham, sour cream, and chopped scallions.

Yield: 15 servings.

Corn & Vidalia Chowder

- 1/2 lb. butter
- 1/2 lb. all-purpose flour
- 1/2 gal. milk
- 2 lb. frozen corn kernels
- 2 Vidalia onions, julienned
- 1/4 lb. chicken bouillon
- 1 pt. heavy whipped cream
- 3 large white potatoes, peeled and diced small
- Salt and pepper to taste

In a 2-gallon pot, melt butter over low heat. Add flour and whisk until it makes a pasty roux. Add milk and cream, bringing to a boil. Simmer for 5 minutes. Add remaining ingredients. Simmer an additional 15 minutes until potatoes soften.

Yield: 15 servings.

Crawfish Chowder

- 1/2 cup onion, chopped
- 1 cup celery, diced
- 1 cup green bell pepper, diced
- 8 tomatoes, seeded and diced
- 2 cups tomato juice
- 1 qt. water, fish stock, or crawfish stock
- 1/2 lb. bacon, diced
- 2 lb. crawfish tail meat
- 2 Tbsp. black pepper
- 6 bay leaves
- 1/4 cup seafood base or salt
- 1/4 cup Thyme
- 1 oz. Tabasco sauce
- 1/3 cup cornstarch

Using a 4-quart stock pot, sauté bacon until browned. Add diced vegetables and sauté in bacon fat until tender. Add the remaining ingredients, except the cornstarch. Simmer 30 minutes. Mix cornstarch with 3 tablespoons water to dissolve, and add to soup as a thickening agent.

Yield: 12 servings.

Oyster Chowder

1/2 lb.	bacon, diced small
1/2	large onion, diced fine
1/2	stalk celery, diced medium
1 qt.	fish stock
1 qt.	oysters
1/2 gal.	milk
1 qt.	heavy cream
2 Tbsp.	white pepper
1 oz.	Tabasco sauce
1 Tbsp.	thyme
4	large potatoes, diced medium
5 oz.	fish or clam base
	Salt to taste

In a 2-gallon pot, cook bacon until well cooked, then add onions and celery. Cook 5 minutes. Next, add milk, stock, cream, juice from a quart of oysters, and all spices. Bring to a boil; thicken with cornstarch. Add oysters and potatoes last.

Yield: 15 servings.

Quail Consommé

Quail Stock

2 lb.	quail bones and skin
1	carrot
1/4	stalk celery
1	small onion
2 qt.	water
2 tsp.	salt
1 tsp.	pepper
1 tsp.	rosemary

In a 3-quart stock pot, lightly cook bones and skin with vegetables. Let it sweat for 15 minutes, then add water and seasoning, simmering for 2 hours. Strain and chill.

Raft

1/2 lb.	ground chuck
8	egg whites
1/2 cup	tomato juice
1/4 cup	carrots, diced
1/4 cup	celery, diced
1/4 cup	onion, diced

Mix raft in proper size mixing bowl and add this mixture to the chilled quail stock, mixing well. Bring this mixture to a slow boil and reduce heat to a slight simmer. Cook for about 10 minutes. Remove raft and strain through a cheesecloth. The broth should have a clear amber color (similar to the color of hot tea).

Yield: 1 quart.

Seafood Chowder

1	large onion, diced
1/2	celery stalk
3	green bell peppers, diced
1 qt.	diced tomatoes
1 (46 oz.)	can tomato juice
1 gal.	fish stock
1 lb.	bacon, diced, cooked (save bacon fat)
1 lb.	70–90 count shrimp, diced
1 lb.	scallops, diced
1 lb.	fish (boneless)
1 Tbsp.	black pepper
2	bay leaves
2 Tbsp.	thyme
2 oz.	Tabasco sauce
	Cornstarch and water slurry

In 2-gallon heavy pot, add all ingredients except cornstarch. Bring mixture to a boil, then simmer for 20 minutes. Thicken with a cornstarch and water slurry. Add salt or fish boullion to taste.

Yield: 15 servings.

Shrimp Gazpacho

2 lb.	fresh tomatoes
1	small onion
1	green bell pepper
1	large cucumber
2 cups	tomato juice
1/8 cup	cider vinegar
1/8 cup	sugar
1 tsp.	garlic, chopped
1/2 lb.	small shrimp
1/2 tsp.	oregano
4	bay leaves
1/2 tsp.	salt
1/2 tsp.	black pepper

Poach shrimp, then chill and peel. Peel and dice tomatoes. Purée cucumber, onion, and bell pepper. Mix with remaining ingredients. Chill for 12 hours.

Yield: 12 servings.

Wild Mushroom & Rice Soup

1/2	large onion, diced fine
1/2	stock celery, diced fine
2 cups	wild rice, raw (pure—not mixed)
2 lb.	wild mushrooms, cut coarse
1/2 cup	cornstarch
1 Gal	Duck Stock (see below)*

Add onion and celery to stock. Bring to a boil and thicken with cornstarch mixed with cold water. Add wild rice and wild mushrooms and simmer 20 minutes longer. Adjust flavor with chicken base and regular ground black pepper.

Duck Stock *

1 gal.	water
3 lb.	duck bones and scraps
1	large carrot
1/2	stalk celery
1	large white onion
2	bay leaves
1 Tbsp.	whole black pepper

Bring to a boil and simmer for 1 hour. Strain with colander.

Yield: 3 quarts.

Wisconsin Cheddar Cheese Soup

1 cup	celery, chopped medium
1 cup	white onion, chopped medium
2	carrots, chopped medium
1/2 lb.	margarine
1/2 lb.	flour
1 qt.	milk
1 qt.	heavy cream
1 qt.	duck or chicken stock
2 lb.	Cheddar cheese

Sauté vegetables with margarine until tender. Add flour, then milk, cream, and stock. Bring to a boil, then add seasonings and cheese.

Yield: 12 servings.

Brown Stock

5 lb.	beef or veal bones
1 lb.	carrots
1 lb.	celery
1 lb.	onions
1	bay leaf
1 Tbsp.	thyme
1 Tbsp.	basil
1 Tbsp.	rosemary
1 tsp.	clove
1/4 cup	whole black pepper
1 cup	tomato paste or #10 can diced tomatoes
2 gallons	water

In a 400° oven, roast bones and vegetables for 30–40 minutes until dark brown. Using 3-gallon pot, combine all ingredients and simmer for 3–4 hours. Strain and thicken with roux of browned butter and flour.

Yield: 1 gallon.

Chicken Stock

5 lb.	chicken bones (may be removed from cooked or raw chicken)
2	medium carrots, washed and quartered
2	medium onions, washed and quartered
2	stalks celery, washed and quartered
2½ qt.	water

Place all ingredients in a large stock pot and bring to a boil. Reduce heat and let simmer undisturbed for 3–5 hours. Remove from heat and strain through a fine sieve. Discard solids and chill liquid, uncovered, overnight. Fat will rise to the top of stock and solidify. This will seal in the stock and preserve it for up to 1 week under refrigeration. Remove fat when ready for use.

Yield: 2 quarts.

Fish Stock

5 lb.	cleaned bones from white fleshed fish (grouper, tile, flounder, etc.)
2	stalks celery, washed and quartered
1	medium onion, peeled, rinsed, and quartered
2 qt.	water

Combine all ingredients in a heavy stockpot. Bring to a boil. Reduce heat and simmer for 30 minutes. Remove from heat and strain through a fine sieve. Discard all solids and chill liquid uncovered.

Yield: 2 quarts.

Tomato Stock

1 quart	chicken stock (home-made or canned)
2 cups	fresh tomatoes, diced
1 cup	white wine*
1 cup	tomato juice
1 tsp.	garlic, chopped
3	Bay Leaves
1	dash Tabasco™ Sauce
1 tsp.	thyme
1 Tbsp.	olive oil
	Salt and Pepper to taste
1/4 cup	corn starch
1/2 cup	cold water

In a medium size pot, sauté garlic in one tablespoon of olive oil, add all ingredients (except corn starch and cold water) bring to a boil and simmer for 20 minutes. In a small bowl, add corn starch and cold water to make a slurry, stir until dissolved. Slowly whisk the slurry into the pot, stir until the stock thickens.

Do not use a cooking wine.

Yield: 2 quarts.

82 Queen Hollandaise

12	egg yolks
½ tsp.	salt
	Juice of 2 lemons
2 cups	butter, clarified, room temperature
4 oz.	water
¼ tsp.	white pepper
3	dashes of Tabasco sauce

Combine all ingredients, except butter, in a large stainless steel bowl. Whip over double boiler until it has consistency of light custard. Do not overcook. Remove from heat and whisk in butter.

Variations:

For dill hollandaise, substitute dill pickle juice for water and add fresh dill.

To make choron, substitute tomato juice for water and add fresh, diced tomato.

For béarnaise, reduce ⅓ cup fresh tarragon with 1 cup vinegar and 2 shallots.

To make orange hollandaise, substitute orange juice for water and add finely chopped orange rind.

Other examples include chili hollandaise (see Page 74), green onion hollandaise, caper hollandaise, lime hollandaise, and shallot hollandaise.

Yield: 12 servings.

A Good Egg

An egg is an egg, right? Wrong! The Charleston area is blessed with eggs produced at Mepkin Abbey, a heavenly outpost located just a few miles north of the city. In 1949, 29 monks from the Abbey in the South Carolina Lowcountry. Commonly called Trappists, the monks belong to the worldwide Order of Cistercians of the Strict Observance. At the abbey, located in Moncks Corner, the monks struggle to live a communal of prayer, sacred reading, and work in an environment of poverty, solitude, and simplicity. They raise and sell eggs to help support the abbey and its charitable endeavors. By the way, the average person in the United States consumes 23 dozen eggs per year.

Basil Cream Sauce

- 4 oz. butter
- 4 oz. flour
- 1 qt. milk
- 1 Tbsp. butter
- 1 cup heavy cream
- 2 oz. chicken base
- 1/2 cup white wine
- 1/4 cup onion, diced fine
- 1/4 cup basil, chopped
- 1 Tbsp. garlic, chopped
- Salt and white pepper to taste

In a saucepan, melt butter over low heat. Add flour and whisk until it makes a pasty roux. Add milk, cream, and white wine. Bring to boil, then reduce to a simmer. Simmer for 10–15 minutes until mixture thickens. Sauté onions and garlic in butter, then add to mixture. Add remaining ingredients and simmer 2 more minutes.

Yield: 1 quart.

Basil Tartar Sauce

- 1 qt. mayonnaise
- 1/2 cup onion, diced fine
- 2 large dill pickles, diced fine
- 1/4 cup fresh basil, chopped fine or puréed
- Juice of 1 fresh lemon
- 1/2 tsp. white pepper
- Dash dry mustard

Combine all ingredients in a large mixing bowl. Blend well. Can be made and stored in refrigerator for 2–3 months.

Yield: 1 quart.

Black Bean Sauce

1/2 lb.	black beans
2 oz.	chili powder
2 oz.	cumin
2 oz.	balsamic vinegar
1 oz.	garlic, chopped
2 qt.	water
1 Tbsp.	black pepper
2 Tbsp.	ham base
2 oz.	olive oil

Combine all ingredients and cook until beans are very tender. Purée. Return to heat and cook until desired consistency.

Yield: 1 quart.

Bourbon Cream

For veal, seafood, or pork

3 oz.	bourbon
2 tsp.	olive oil
1/3 cup	shallots
1/2 cup	pecans, chopped
2 Tbsp.	brown sugar
1 qt.	heavy cream
	Salt and white pepper to taste

Heat 2-quart saucepan on medium heat and add oil. Let oil heat for 1 minute, then add shallots and chopped pecans to hot oil. Cook until shallots are transparent. Add brown sugar and mix while on heat, then add bourbon to deglaze the pan. Burn off alcohol by lighting bourbon with a match or open gas flame. When the flames burn out, add cream and reduce by half. Add salt and white pepper to taste.

Yield: 8 servings.

Charleston Spiced Mayonnaise

6	eggs
2 Tbsp.	vinegar
½ tsp.	salt
¼ tsp.	sugar
½ tsp.	white pepper
1 tsp.	Dijon mustard
4 cups	salad oil
¼ cup	parsley
1 tsp.	cayenne pepper
2 tsp.	mace
1 tsp.	granulated garlic
3 tsp.	lemon juice

In a stainless steel or glass bowl, combine eggs, mustard, and vinegar; whisk well. Add oil very slowly until it is all blended (the mixture should be very thick). Add all remaining ingredients.

Yield: 1 quart.

Cherry Grand Marnier Glaze

1½ cups	Grand Marnier
1 (60 oz.)	bottle cranberry juice
3 cups	sugar
1 tsp.	ground cinnamon
4	cinnamon sticks
1 oz.	Tabasco sauce
½ tsp.	salt
2 oz.	orange concentrate
3 lbs.	sun-dried cherries
¼ cup	cornstarch
⅛ cup	water

In large saucepan, combine all ingredients except cherries. Let simmer 20 minutes. Add cherries and simmer 15 more minutes. Thicken with slurry of cornstarch and water.

Yield: 20 servings.

Chili Hollandaise

1	red bell pepper, diced fine
1	shallot, diced fine
1 Tbsp.	garlic, minced
1	green bell pepper, diced fine
1	tomato, diced fine
	Olive oil
1/2 cup	white wine
1/4 tsp.	gumbo filé
	Dash of cayenne pepper
1/2 tsp.	chili powder
1 pt.	82 Queen Hollandaise

Sauté red pepper, shallot, garlic, green pepper, and tomato in olive oil. Add white wine, gumbo filé, cayenne pepper, and chili powder. Reduce to one-third. Let cool to room temperature and add to 82 Queen Hollandaise (see Page 70).

Yield: 1 pint.

Cocktail Sauce

14 oz.	ketchup
8 oz.	chili sauce
1/2 cup	horseradish
1 oz.	Tabasco sauce
1/4 cup	lemon juice
2 oz.	Worcestershire sauce
1 Tbsp.	black pepper

Combine ingredients and mix well.

Yield: 8–12 servings.

Cranberry & Apricot Glaze

2 qt.	cranberry juice
1 (6 oz.)	can orange juice concentrate
2 cups	sugar
1 cup	cider vinegar
3	cinnamon sticks
1 tsp.	ground cinnamon
1 Tbsp.	salt
1 lb.	dried apricots, julienned
1 lb.	dried cranberries

Combine ingredients and simmer until desired consistency.

Yield: 2 quarts.

Field Pea Sauce

1 lb.	field peas (dry)
4 oz.	ham base
7 oz.	balsamic vinegar
2 tsp.	soy sauce
1 tsp.	cayenne
1 tsp.	salt
1/2 tsp.	white pepper
4 oz.	brown sugar
2 qt.	water

Combine all ingredients. Simmer for 1 hour. Strain peas and retain liquid. Purée peas and add back to liquid. Cook 20 minutes until slightly thick.

Yield: 1 quart.

Peas Please

Gardening was among the favorite pastimes of U.S. President Thomas Jefferson. The founding father's garden featured some 15 types of English peas, which was considered his favorite vegetable. His frequent writings in his garden book suggest that he paid particular attention to the vegetable, noting in detail when "peas come to the table." By staggering the planting of his peas, Jefferson was able to enjoy them from the middle of May to the middle of July. What else did Jefferson enjoy? Wine. It is reported that he spent about $2,000 a year on wine. In today" dollars that would be about $18,000 each year.

Herb Seasoning Blend

3/4 cup	dry basil leaves, crumbled
1/2 cup	dry oregano leaves, crumbled
1/4 cup	onion powder
2 Tbsp.	garlic powder

Combine all ingredients. Can be used to season chicken, pork, veal, and beef.

Yield: 1 1/2 cups.

Honey & Ginger Dipping Sauce

8 oz.	jar pure honey
4 oz.	Dijon mustard
2 tsp.	fresh grated ginger

Combine ingredients in small bowl and mix well.

Yield: 2 cups.

Jalapeño Cocktail Sauce

1/4 cup	diced jalapeño peppers
3 oz.	green Tabasco sauce
14 oz.	ketchup
12 oz.	chili sauce
1/4 cup	horseradish
1/4 cup	lemon juice
2 oz.	Worcestershire sauce
1 tsp.	black pepper

Combine all ingredients and mix well.

Yield: 12–15 servings.

Jambalaya Sauce

1½ oz.	margarine
1½ oz.	flour
1 cup	tomato juice
1 qt.	fish stock
1 tsp.	lemon juice
1 tsp.	crushed black pepper
½ tsp.	crushed red pepper
1 Tbsp.	garlic, chopped
1 Tbsp.	salt
½ tsp.	thyme
½ tsp.	basil
½ tsp.	oregano

In a 2-quart saucepan, melt margarine over low heat. Add flour to margarine and whisk until it makes a pasty roux. Add fish stock and whisk until roux is dissolved. Add all other ingredients and increase heat to high. Whisk thoroughly until sauce comes to a full boil. Remove from heat. Sauce may be stored overnight or served immediately.

Yield: 1½ quarts.

Orange Pepper Marmalade

1 (8 oz.) jar	orange marmalade
3 Tbsp.	Tiger Sauce (hot pepper sauce)

Using heavy sauce pot, bring marmalade to a boil. Add Tiger Sauce and cook for two minutes. Remove from heat and chill. Best served at room temperature. Store up to three months in refrigerator.

Yield: 8 servings.

Pesto

1/2 lb.	basil
1 cup	pine nuts
2 cups	olive oil
1/4 cup	garlic, chopped
1/2 cup	grated Parmesan cheese
1 tsp.	white pepper
2 tsp.	salt

Purée all ingredients in blender.

Yield: 1 quart.

Praline Bourbon Glaze

2 cups	bourbon
2 cups	water
1/4 lb.	brown sugar
1/2 cup	orange juice
1/4 tsp.	white pepper
1/4 tsp.	salt
1/4 tsp.	ground cinnamon
2 Tbsp.	cornstarch

In heavy saucepan, bring bourbon to boil for 5 minutes. Carefully light bourbon so that it flames in pot to burn off alcohol (should take about 2 minutes). Add all other ingredients except cornstarch. Bring to boil. Thicken sauce with cornstarch-water slurry. Serve hot or at room temperature.

Yield: 12 servings.

Raspberry Orange Sauce

  1 cup sugar
  1 lb. raspberries
 1/4 cup orange juice concentrate
 1/4 cup orange rind, julienned
  3 tsp. raspberry vinegar
  1 cup water
  1 tsp. cinnamon

Bring water and sugar to boil. Reduce by one-fourth. Add remaining ingredients and simmer for 10 minutes. Thicken slightly with cornstarch.

                Yield: 12 servings.

Red Pepper Sauce
For shrimp, scallops, seafood sausage, and most fish

  4 oz. flour
  4 oz. margarine
 2 cups milk
 2 cups fish stock
    2 red bell peppers, roasted, seeded, and peeled
 1/4 tsp. cayenne pepper
     Salt and white pepper to taste
 1/4 cup sherry wine
  1 tsp. paprika
 1/4 cup bacon fat

In a saucepan, melt margarine over low heat. Add flour and whisk until it makes a pasty roux. Add milk, fish stock, and sherry. Bring to boil, then reduce heat and simmer. Add puréed red peppers (roasted, seeded, and peeled). Add remaining ingredients. Let simmer 10 minutes and strain through medium-fine sieve. If sauce looks too thick, add more milk.

                Yield: 6 servings.

Sweet Red Pepper Coulis

4	large red peppers
1/2 tsp.	White Pepper
1 tsp.	Apple Cider Vinegar
3 tsp.	honey
3	large shallots
1 Tbsp.	olive oil
1 cup	water

Seed and dice red peppers; peel and chop shallots. Pre-heat a medium size sauté pan, add olive oil, sauté shallots for 30 seconds, then add red peppers and sauté for 3 more minutes (or until soft), then add water. Simmer for 10 minutes. Pour mixture into a medium size bowl then add remaining ingredients. Using an immersion blender, blend mixture until smooth. Set mixture aside to cool at room temperature.

Yield: 2 cups.

Soy Dipping Sauce

2 cups	water
1 cup	soy
8 oz.	brown sugar
1 oz.	fresh ginger, chopped fine
2 Tbsp.	cornstarch

In medium sauce pan, bring water, soy, brown sugar, and ginger to a boil. Add a slurry of cornstarch and water to thicken. Simmer 10 minutes.

Yield: 8–10 servings.

Tasso Gravy

1/4 lb.	margarine
1	onion, chopped
2	stalks celery, chopped
1 lb.	tasso ham, diced
1/4 cup	flour
2 cups	ham or chicken stock
1 oz.	thyme
1 cup	heavy cream
	Kitchen bouquet
	Salt and black pepper to taste

Sauté vegetables and tasso ham. Stir in flour. Add stock and bring to a boil. Reduce heat and continue cooking until thickened. Add thyme, heavy cream, and kitchen bouquet. Adjust seasoning as needed.

Yield: 12–15 servings.

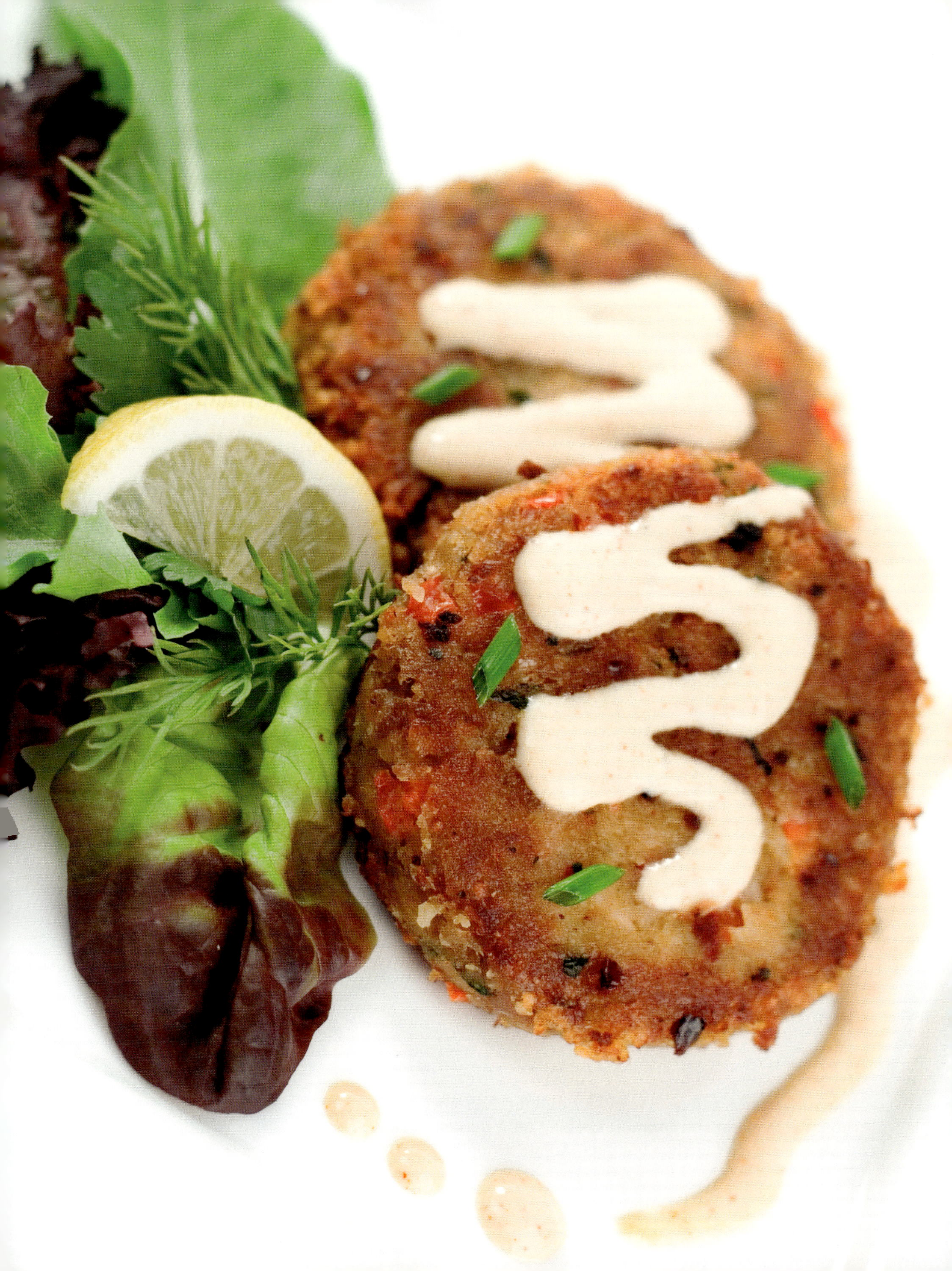

SEAFOOD

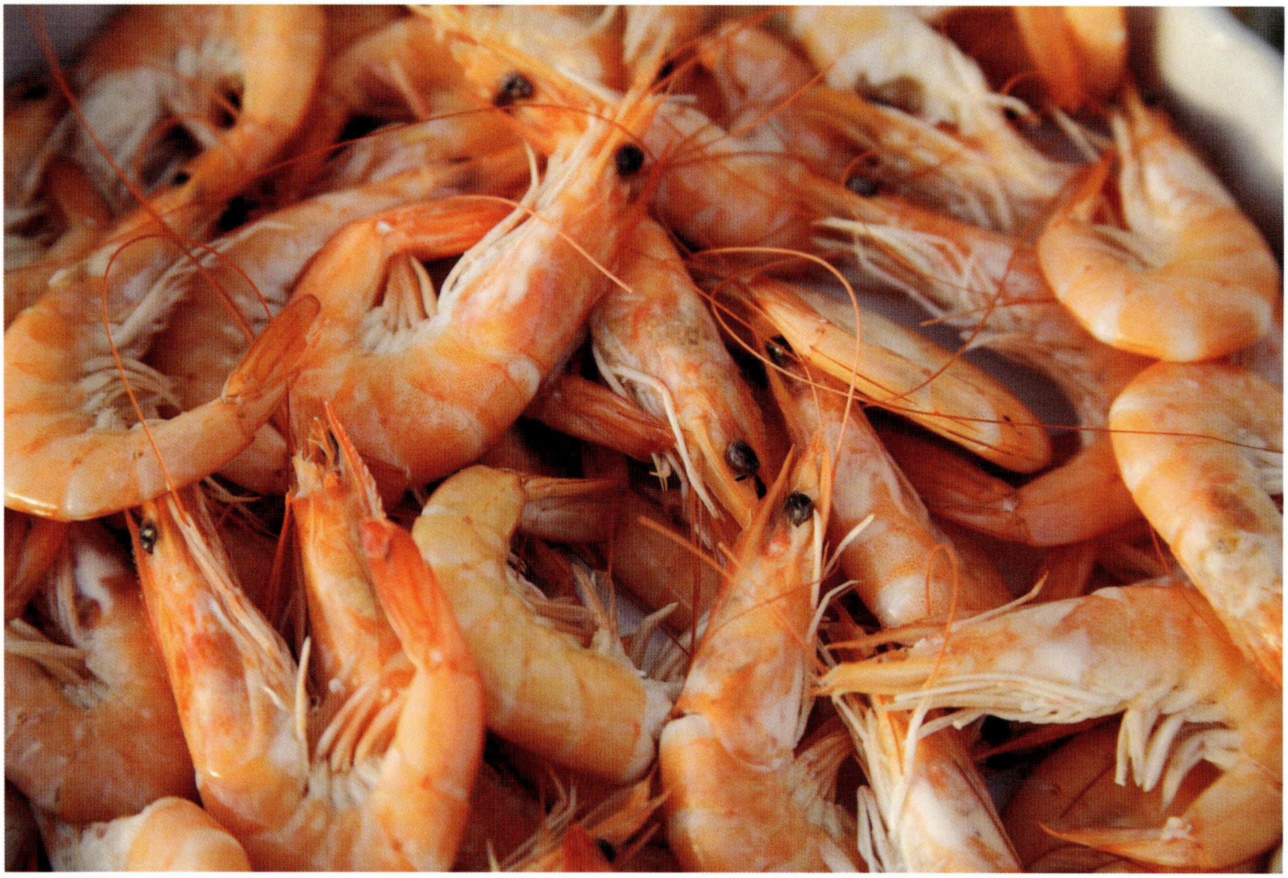

Seafood

82 Queen Crabmeat Imperial ... 91

Charleston Crabmeat Boil ... 91

82 Queen World Famous Crab Cakes with Sweet Red Pepper Coulis ... 92

Crawfish & Shirmp Cake ... 93

Daufuskie Deviled Crab ... 94

Fresh Catch in Parchment Paper ... 95

Frogmore Stew ... 96

Grilled American Red Snapper with Tomato Coulis ... 97

Grilled Sea Scallops over Sweet Pepper & Cilantro Coulis ... 98

Grilled Shrimp & Prosciutto with Brie Cheese Sauce ... 99

Grouper en Papilotte à l'Orange ... 100

Jambalaya ... 100

Oyster Gumbo ... 101

Sautéed Shrimp & Scallops in Creamed Spinach & Tomato ... 102

Seafood Quiche ... 103

Toogoodoo Vegetables & Shrimp in Parchment Paper ... 103

Providing 82 Queen with the Lowcountry's Freshest Seafood for more than 20 years.

CROSBY'S SEAFOOD INC.

Get your fresh seafood at Crosby's Downtown Store
located at the intersection
of Lockwood Boulevard and Spring Street.

Call (843) 937-0029

382 Spring Street - Charleston, SC 29403

Open 9:00am to 6:00pm - 7 Days a Week
Coming Soon! www.crosbysseafood.com

82 Queen Crabmeat Imperial

1 lb.	crabmeat, picked
3	slices white bread
1/2	onion
1/2	green bell pepper
1 Tbsp.	pimentos, diced
1 Tbsp.	parsley
1	lemon, juiced
1/4 tsp.	dry mustard
1/4 tsp.	Worcestershire sauce
1 cup	mayonnaise
	Salt and pepper to taste
	Tabasco sauce to taste

Sauté peppers and onions until half-done. Cut bread into small cubes. Combine all ingredients and toss lightly. Bake casserole at 325° for 30 minutes. This imperial mix can be used to stuff shrimp, flounder, clams, etc., or placed in a casserole dish as an entrée.

Yield: 4 servings.

Charleston Crabmeat Boil

2	English muffins, toasted
4	tomato slices
4	slices Swiss cheese
4 oz.	82 Queen Crabmeat Imperial

Place crabmeat mix on each muffin half and top with sliced tomato, then Swiss cheese. Bake at 450° for 12–15 minutes.

Yield: 2 servings.

Note: 82 Queen World-Famous BBQ Shrimp & Grits Page 50

82 Queen World Famous Crab Cakes with Sweet Red Pepper Coulis

1 lb.	lump crabmeat
1/2 cup	mayonnaise
2	green onions, chopped fine
2	dashes of Tabasco sauce
1	dash of Worcestershire sauce
1/2 cup	coarse bread crumbs
1/2 oz.	fresh lemon juice
2	eggs
1/4 cup	Half & Half cream
	Butter or olive oil

Combine all ingredients except eggs and Half & Half thoroughly, then form into desired cake shape (about 4 ounces). Combine eggs and Half & Half to make an egg wash. Dip cakes in wash, then roll in more bread crumbs. Sauté in butter or olive oil until golden brown.

Sweet Red Pepper Coulis

4	large red bell peppers, seeded and diced medium
1/2 tsp.	white pepper
1 tsp.	apple cider vinegar
3 tsp.	honey
3	large shallots, peeled and chopped
1/2 cup	water

Sauté bell peppers and shallots together. Add water and simmer 20 minutes or until peppers are soft completely through. Using a high-speed blender, mix peppers, shallots, and all remaining ingredients in a bowl and blend until smooth. Run through a medium strainer. Set aside at room temperature.

Yield: 6 cakes.

Crawfish & Shrimp Cake

1 lb.	crawfish tail meat, cooked
1 lb.	cooked shrimp
1/2 cup	large red bell pepper, chopped fine
1/4 cup	green onions, chopped fine
2 oz.	lemon juice
1/2 cup	mayonnaise
1 tsp.	Tabasco sauce
1 tsp.	Cajun spice
1/2 tsp.	salt
1/4 tsp.	white pepper
1 cup	breadcrumbs
4	eggs
1 cup	milk

Poach shrimp and chill in cold water. Drain well, then roughly chop up shrimp and crawfish. Add red pepper, green onion, lemon juice, mayonnaise, Tabasco, Cajun spice, salt, and white pepper. Adjust tightness and consistency with bread crumbs. Season to taste. Make egg wash by mixing eggs and milk. Weigh out 3½-oz. portions and bread by dipping in egg wash and rolling in bread crumbs. Pan fry in hot oil or butter, cooking 2 minutes each side. Finish in 375–400° oven for 10 minutes.

Yield: 12 cakes.

Daufuskie Deviled Crab

1 lb.	white crabmeat
1	medium onion, diced fine
2	celery sticks, diced fine
1 cup	mayonnaise
¼ cup	ketchup
1 Tbsp.	lemon juice
1 tsp.	Tabasco sauce
	Salt to taste
1 lb.	claw meat
1	green bell pepper, diced fine
1 tsp.	garlic
½ cup	yellow mustard
1 Tbsp.	Worcestershire sauce
1 cup	bread crumbs
½ tsp.	cayenne pepper

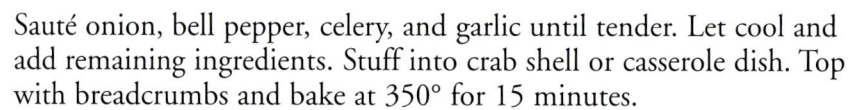

Sauté onion, bell pepper, celery, and garlic until tender. Let cool and add remaining ingredients. Stuff into crab shell or casserole dish. Top with breadcrumbs and bake at 350° for 15 minutes.

Yield: 10–12 filled shells.

Off to Market

The market in downtown Charleston has been a primary shopping district in the city for nearly 200 years. Stretching from East Bay Street all the way to Meeting Street, the market was built on land given to the City of Charleston for a public market in the 18th century by Charles Coatesworth Pinckney, a signer of the Declaration of Independence. Today, the vendors include many local artisans and importers who occupy both the open-air market and the adjoining enclosed Rainbow Market. Locally grown produce is also sold in the open-air market. Charleston, reluctant to let go of her history. In addition to the produce sold daily at the market, the City of Charleston also sponsors a farmers market near Marion Square on Saturday mornings April through October.

Fresh Catch in Parchment Paper

    2 (7 oz.) portions fresh fish (preferably a flaky white fish)
    2 sheets parchment paper (12 x 20 inches)
    Oil
    Marinade

Add fish fillet to marinade and let stand for 20 minutes. Place marinated fillet on parchment paper that has been lightly oiled. Fold in half and fold outside edges to form a completely sealed bag. Bake at 400° for 15–20 minutes.

Marinade
    2 oz. red onion, julienned
    2 tsp. balsamic vinegar
    1 tsp. dill, chopped
    1 oz. capers
    2 tsp. olive oil
    2 tsp. lemon juice
    Dash cracked black pepper

In a mixing bowl, combine all marinade ingredients and mix well.

Yield: 2 servings.

Frogmore Stew

1 lb.	shrimp (30 count), peeled
2 lb.	chicken breast, boneless, skinless and grilled
1 lb.	andouille hot sausage, sliced
1 cup	celery, diced large
½ cup	onion, diced large
1 cup	mixed bell peppers (red, yellow, green)
½ cup	kernel corn
6 cups	cooked white rice
	Tomato stock

Sauté vegetables in large heavy skillet, using ¼ cup oil, until vegetables are half-cooked. Add remaining ingredients, except rice, and sauté for 5 minutes. Add tomato stock ingredients and simmer for 10 minutes. Thicken with cornstarch-water slurry. Serve over white rice.

Tomato Stock (home method)

3 cups	V-8 juice
2	bay leaves
2 Tbsp.	brown sugar
1 tsp.	thyme
2 tsp.	cornstarch (mixed with 2 tsp. water)
	Salt and black pepper to taste

Yield: 6 servings.

The Lowdown on Lowcountry Cuisine

Exactly what is Lowcountry cuisine? Like New Orleans cuisine, a multitude of influences spice the Lowcountry pot. Blending French, English, Spanish, African, Caribbean, and many other cultures, the "melting pot" phenomenon made its way into stove pots across the region. In Lowcountry cuisine, seafood is probably the first food that comes to mind. But more specifically, think gumbo, jambalaya, and crab cakes. Then toss in some rice, beans, and definitely spices for an unusual face availability only in South Carolina's Lowcountry.

Grilled American Red Snapper with Tomato Coulis

4 (7–8 oz.)	red snapper fillets
2 tsp.	fresh lemon juice
	Salt and white pepper to taste
	Thyme butter (*see below)
4	bunches arugula, lightly washed
	Tomato coulis (** see below)
4	stems fresh thyme

Wash fillets and pat dry with towel; season with fresh lemon, salt, and white pepper. Sprinkle apple chips that have been soaked in water on coals prior to cooking. Grill snapper over bed of hot coals (mesquite or charcoal briquettes). Baste fillets with thyme butter while grilling. Serve grilled fillets over blanched bed of arugula. Top snapper with tomato coulis and garnish plate with fresh thyme.

Thyme Butter *

1/2 cup	fresh thyme
2 Tbsp.	shallots, diced fine
1/2 tsp.	salt
1 lb.	butter
2 Tbsp.	lemon juice
1/4 tsp.	white pepper

Sauté shallots until transparent. Add butter and remaining ingredients. Blend well. Electric mixer can be used.

Tomato Coulis **

2	large fresh tomatoes
1/3 cup	red wine vinegar
1/3 cup	red onion, diced fine
2 Tbsp.	fresh thyme, chopped
2 Tbsp.	fresh arugula, chopped
1 tsp.	lemon juice
1/2 tsp.	sugar
1/4 tsp.	salt
1/4 tsp.	pepper

Poach tomatoes 30 seconds in boiling water; remove skin and seeds and dice medium to fine. Add all remaining ingredients. Let marinate 2 hours before serving.

Yield: 4 servings.

Grilled Sea Scallops with Sweet Pepper & Cilantro Coulis

30	sea scallops (20–30 count)
2 Tbsp.	olive oil
2 oz.	balsamic vinegar
1 Tbsp.	brown sugar
1/2 tsp.	white pepper
1/2 tsp.	cayenne pepper
1 tsp.	cumin
1 tsp.	chili powder
1/2 tsp.	garlic, chopped fine
1/4 cup	water
	Sweet pepper & cilantro coulis

Lightly poach scallops. Add remaining ingredients, except coulis, into a medium-size bowl and mix well using a whisk. Add scallops and let sit for a minimum of ½ hour. Grill scallops on hot gas or charcoal grill (only 1 minute per side) and arrange on a bed of coulis. Garnish with shoestring vegetables and low calorie sour cream.

Sweet Pepper & Cilantro Coulis

4	large red bell peppers
3 tsp.	chopped cilantro
1/2 tsp.	white pepper
1 tsp.	apple cider vinegar
3 tsp.	honey
3	large shallots
1 Tbsp.	olive oil
1/2 cup	water

Seed and dice red peppers (medium dice). Peel and chop shallots. Sauté peppers and shallots together in olive oil and ½ cup water. Simmer for 20 minutes or until peppers are soft completely through. Place peppers, shallots, and all remaining ingredients (except cilantro) in a bowl. Using a high-speed blender, blend until smooth, then run through a medium strainer. Add cilantro and set aside at room temperature.

Yield: 4–6 servings.

Grilled Shrimp & Prosciutto with Brie Cheese Sauce

24	large shrimp
1/2 cup	olive oil
1/4 cup	white wine
1/4 cup	lemon juice
1/4 cup	fresh basil
1 tsp.	garlic, chopped
1 tsp.	sugar
	Salt and pepper to taste
1/2 lb.	prosciutto ham
1	whole lemon
	Brie cheese sauce (*see below)

Peel, clean, and rinse shrimp. For marinade, chop basil and add to olive oil, white wine, lemon juice, garlic, and sugar. Salt and pepper to taste. Chill shrimp for 2 hours in marinade mixture. Slice prosciutto into 16 very thin slices about 1 inch wide and 3 inches long. Cut lemon in 12 wedges. Wrap prosciutto around shrimp and put 4 on a skewer alternating with 3 lemon wedges. Grill shrimp over hot coals with mesquite chips. Baste with marinade during grilling. Serve grilled shrimp on bed of spinach. Top with Brie cheese sauce and toasted pine nuts. Serve with a side of fresh pasta or rice.

Brie Cheese Sauce*

1/2 lb.	butter
1/2 lb.	flour
1/2 lb.	Brie cheese, skinned
1 pt.	milk
2	dashes of Tabasco sauce
	Salt and white pepper to taste

In a saucepan, melt butter over low heat. Add flour and whisk until it makes a pasty roux. Add milk and whisk. When hot, add Brie and seasoning.

Yield: 4 servings.

Grouper en Papilotte à l'Orange

2 (6 oz.)	grouper (fresh if possible)
1/2 cup	fresh squeezed orange juice
2 tsp.	orange rind
1/4 tsp.	salt
	Dash of white pepper
2	sheet white parchment paper (12 x 20 in.)
1 tsp.	shallots, chopped

Preheat oven to 400°. Cut parchment paper into heart shape and oil both sides. Place the grouper in paper and top with orange juice, rind, and seasoning. Crimp edges closed. Bake 20 minutes.

Yield: 2 servings.

Jambalaya

6 cups	rice (cooked in chicken broth)
1/2 lb.	Andouille sausage, sliced
1 lb.	medium shrimp, peeled
1/2 lb.	crawfish tail-meat
1	large tomato, diced
1	sweet onion, diced
1	red bell pepper, diced
1	yellow bell pepper, diced
2	celery sticks, diced
1/2 tsp.	Old Bay Seasoning
1 tsp.	Cajun blackening spice
1/4 cup	butter
	Salt, pepper, Tabasco sauce to taste

In a large skillet, sauté all ingredients (except rice) until shrimp are cooked. Add rice and stir until well blended. Adjust seasoning and add Tabasco sauce to desired taste.

Yield: 4 servings.

Oyster Gumbo

16	fresh local oysters, shucked and left on the half-shell
½ cup plus 1 Tbsp.	butter (room temperature)
1 Tbsp.	gumbo filé
1 Tbsp.	tomato paste
1 tsp.	fresh thyme
½ tsp.	garlic, chopped fine
½ tsp.	cayenne pepper
	Black pepper and salt to taste
1	red onion, julienned small
1	stalk celery, julienned small
1	red bell pepper, julienned small
½ lb.	smoked ham, julienned small
	Breadcrumb topping (*see below)

Whip filé, tomato paste, thyme, garlic, cayenne pepper, salt, black pepper, and ¼ cup of butter until thoroughly mixed. Divide among oysters on the half-shell. Sauté onion, celery, red pepper and ham in 1 Tbsp. butter until tender. Divide among oysters and bake at 350° for 5 minutes. Sprinkle breadcrumb topping over oysters and continue baking at 350° until browned.

Breadcrumb Topping *

¾ cup	breadcrumbs
1 Tbsp.	butter, melted
½ tsp.	garlic powder
1 tsp.	parsley
	Salt to taste

Toss breadcrumbs with other ingredients.

Yield: 2 entrée servings (4 appetizer servings).

Mumbo, Gumbo

So what is gumbo, exactly? Just about anything you want it to be. Gumbo is a soup or stew that blends the rich cuisines of the French, Spanish, Indian and African Cultures. Derived from the African word "gumbo," which means okra, the word "gumbo" first appeared in print in the early 1800s. The practice of thickening gumbo with filé powder, which is made from the ground, dried leaves of the sassafras tree, was begun about two decades later by the Choctaw Indians from the Louisiana bayou country. There are no hard and fast rules for making gumbo beyond the okra, filé powder, or basic roux, and your imagination.

Seafood

Sautéed Shrimp & Scallops in Creamed Spinach & Tomato

    3 dozen peeled shrimp
    3 dozen scallops
    1/4 cup butter
    1/4 cup white wine

Lightly sauté shrimp and scallops in butter and wine. Smother with prepared creamed spinach and tomato and simmer 5 minutes. Serve over fresh pasta and garnish with shredded Parmesan cheese.

Creamed Spinach & Tomato
    4 oz. butter
    2 cups milk
    4 oz. flour
    2 oz. seafood base
    1 onion, diced fine
    1 Tbsp. garlic, chopped
    1 cup fresh tomatoes, diced
    1 cup heavy cream
    1/2 cup white wine
    2 cups fresh spinach
    Salt to taste
    White pepper to taste

In a saucepan, melt butter over low heat. Add flour and whisk until it makes a pasty roux. Add remaining ingredients. Bring to a boil, stirring constantly. Season and simmer for additional 5 minutes.

Yield: 6–8 servings.

Seafood Quiche

1	(9-inch) pie shell
¼ lb.	scallops
¼ lb.	shrimp, peeled and deveined
¼ lb.	white crabmeat, special
6	eggs
1 cup	milk
1 cup	shredded Cheddar cheese
¼ cup	sherry wine
	Salt and pepper to taste

Arrange raw seafood in pie shell. Mix eggs, milk, sherry, salt, and pepper. Pour over seafood already in pie shell. Top with shredded Cheddar cheese and bake at 375° for 1 hour. Let cool 15 minutes before slicing. You can top with a white wine sauce and/or bacon bits.

Yield: 4 large servings.

Toogoodoo Vegetables & Shrimp in Parchment Paper

4 dozen	large shrimp, peeled and deveined
2	medium zucchini
1	small Vidalia onion
1	red bell pepper
¼ cup	fresh herbs (basil, dill, cilantro, tarragon)
1 Tbsp.	black pepper
1	small yellow squash
16	pieces of fresh okra
4	pieces of parchment paper (12 x 20 in.)
½ cup	olive oil
	Salt to taste

Cut all vegetables into medium size sticks. Toss all ingredients in large mixing bowl. Divide vegetables and shrimp onto 4 pieces of parchment paper and fold paper over, crimping edges to close completely. Bake at 400° for 15–20 minutes.

Yield: 4 servings.

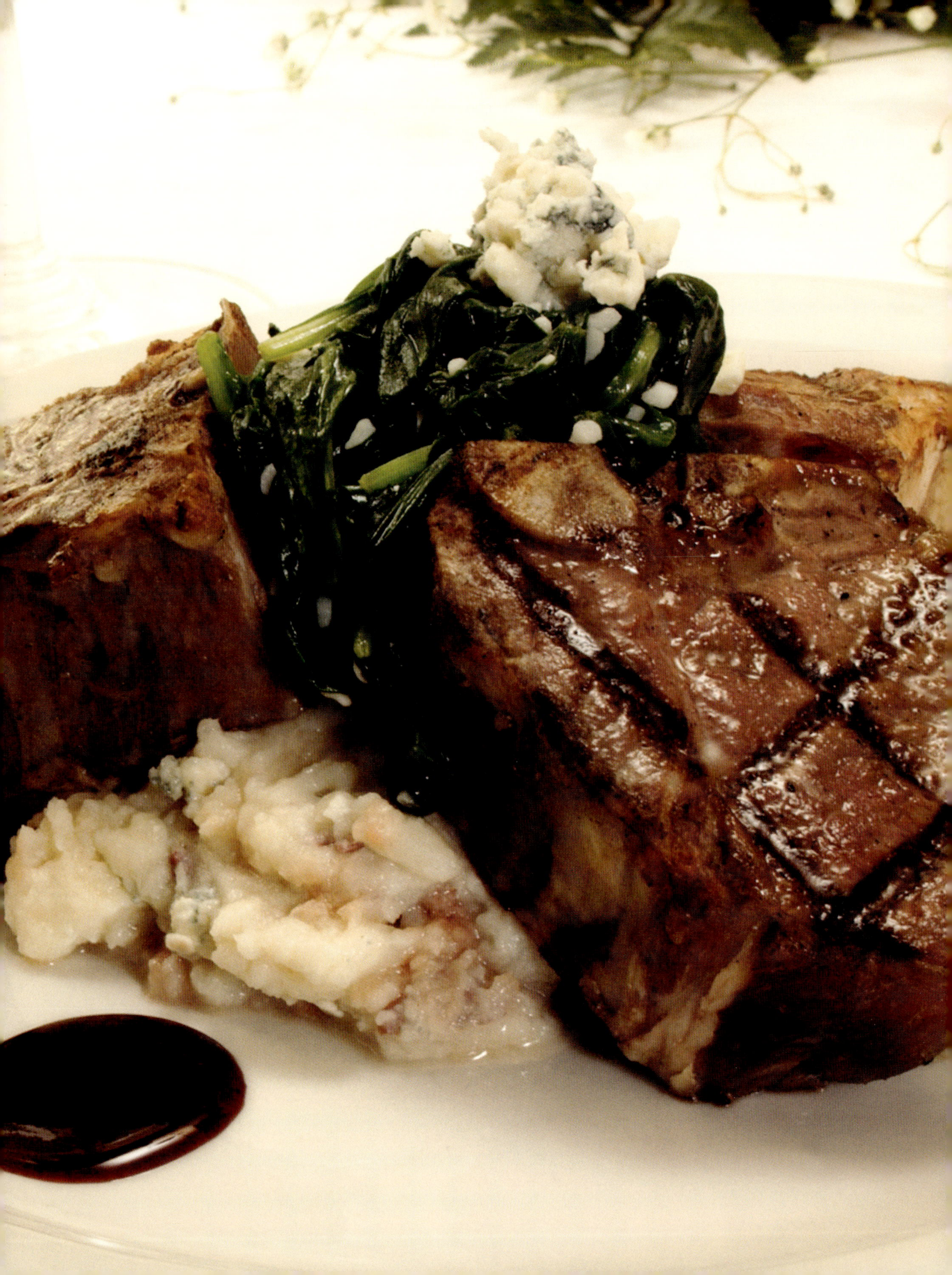

MEAT & FOWL

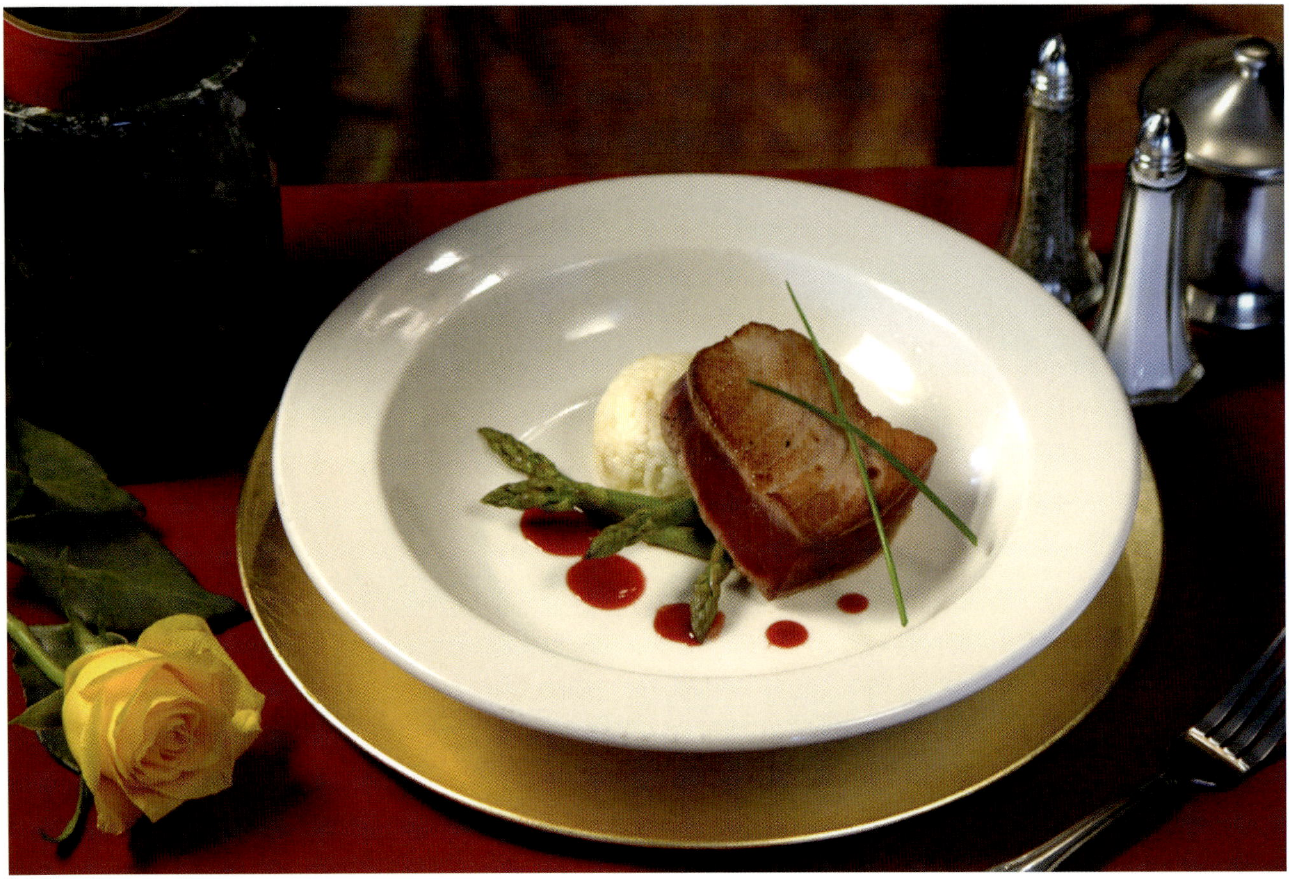

Meat

Beef Jerky ... 108
Count Cristo ... 108
Lowcountry Bourbon & Praline Pork Loin ... 109
Rosemary & Garlic Roasted Pork Loin ... 110

Fowl

82 Queen Lowcountry Salsa Chicken ... 111
Baked Chicken Stuffing ... 111
Chicken & Leeks with Ravioli ... 112
Grilled Brace of Quail with Peanut Sauce ... 113
Mesquite Grilled Pulled Mallard with Apple Cider Glaze ...114
Smoked Wild Turkey ... 115

Beef Jerky

  2 cups Worcestershire sauce
  2 cups teriyaki sauce
  2 cups soy sauce
  8 oz. light brown sugar
  2 Tbsp. black pepper
  4 oz. granulated garlic
  4 oz. Liquid Smoke
  5 Tbsp. salt
  1 Tbsp. ground ginger
  10–15 lb. venison or beef in strips

Combine all ingredients and marinate 24 hours. Dry the marinated meat in a dehydrator or smoker.

Yield: 3–5 pounds dried meat.

Count Cristo

  6 slices bread
  4 oz. (4 slices) cooked ham
  4 oz. cooked turkey
  4 slices Swiss cheese
  3 eggs

Place ham and Swiss cheese on a slice of bread. Cover with another slice of bread and place turkey and Swiss on top of that. Place third slice of bread on top. Trim crusts and cut in half. Hold halves together with toothpicks. Dip each half in beaten egg and deep fry for 1½ minutes. Remove toothpicks before serving.

Yield: 2 servings.

Lowcountry Bourbon & Praline Pork Loin

12 oz.	pork loin, trimmed, tenderized, and cut into 1–2 oz. pieces
2 tsp.	olive oil
2 tsp.	shallots, chopped fine
1/4 cup	pecans, chopped
1/2 cup	heavy cream
1 tsp.	brown sugar
2 oz.	bourbon
2 oz.	plain flour
	Salt & white pepper to taste
	Carolina white rice or fresh cooked pasta

Heat sauté pan on medium heat. Add olive oil. Heat oil one minute, then quickly sauté shallots until they turn light brown. Dust pork lightly with flour and add to pan. Sauté 1–2 minutes per side until golden brown. Add sugar and pecans, and deglaze pan with bourbon. Bourbon should flame, so be careful. When flames disappear, add cream, salt, and white pepper. Reduce by half.

Yield: 2 servings.

Rosemary & Garlic Roasted Pork Loin

3–5 lb.	pork loin
1 cup	oil
1/4 bunch	fresh rosemary, chopped
2 Tbsp.	black pepper
1 Tbsp.	garlic
1 Tbsp.	brown sugar
1 Tbsp.	salt
1 Tbsp.	gravy bouquet
1 Tbsp.	Liquid Smoke

Make a brine of all the ingredients except the pork loin. Marinate the pork loin in the brine overnight. Grill 5 minutes each side, and place in a 350° oven for an additional 15 minutes to cook to medium-rare. Slice and serve with mashed potatoes or mashed sweet potatoes.

Yield: 6–10 servings.

Pig Pickin'

Today, it's not unusual for Southerners to host pig roasts. The popular outdoor event features a pig that has been roasted all day in an open pit and is served with a variety of picnic fare. In 1864, however, the practice wasn't quite as socially acceptable when Gen. William T. Sherman was hosting the event. During his March to the Sea, Sherman frequently fed his 60,000 troops on livestock and crops "appropriated" from rural farms. One of the army's favorites: roasted pig served with sweet potatoes dug up from the fields. History tells us that soldiers of both the Union and Confederate armies were notoriously thorough foragers, and in most marches left the country behind them picked clean.

82 Queen Lowcountry Salsa Chicken

4 (6–7 oz.)	boneless chicken breasts
4 Tbsp.	olive oil
1 tsp.	dry thyme
	Pinch salt
	Johns Island salsa
	Linguini

Add olive oil, thyme, and salt to chicken breasts in bowl and let marinate in refrigerator for a day. Grill chicken until done. Serve over fresh cooked linguine with Johns Island salsa.

Johns Island Salsa

1/2 bunch	cilantro
3	vine ripe farm fresh tomatoes, seeded and chopped
1/2	cucumber, seeded
2 cloves	fresh garlic
1/4	red onion, cut into chunks
1	green bell pepper, cut into chunks
1 Tbsp.	salt
1 Tbsp.	pepper
1 oz.	olive oil
1 Tbsp.	brown sugar
	Tabasco sauce to taste

Mix all ingredients in food processor until fine. Adjust flavor with salt and Tabasco sauce.

Yield: 4 servings.

Baked Chicken Stuffing

1/2 tub	Rondele cheese (herbed cream cheese)
2	eggs
1	bag spinach, chopped
2 cups	mushrooms, chopped
1 tsp.	salt
1 tsp.	white pepper

Combine all ingredients and mix well. Mixture will stuff 10–12 (8 oz.) skinless, boneless chicken breasts.

Yield: 10–12 servings.

Chicken & Leeks with Ravioli

4 (8-oz.)	chicken breasts, grilled and diced
2 lbs.	cheese-filled ravioli or tortellini, cooked
1 cup	leeks, chopped
1 cup	fresh mushrooms, sliced
½ cup	white wine
1 cup	heavy whipping cream
1½–2 cups	milk
	Salt and pepper to taste
1 cube	chicken bouillon
2 oz.	flour
4 cloves	fresh garlic, minced
2 oz.	butter
1 lb.	shredded Parmesan cheese

Lightly sauté leeks in butter. Dust with flour. Add white wine and heavy cream. Add chicken bouillon and half of the milk. Bring to a boil, stirring constantly to prevent scorching or lumping. Add remaining ingredients, except ravioli, and simmer for 5 minutes. Use remaining milk if necessary to thin sauce. Season. Add pre-cooked ravioli and serve topped with Parmesan cheese.

Yield: 4 servings.

Boo! Beware of Ghosts

It is undisputed that Charleston is the most haunted city in the country. While our ghost population has grown through the centuries, vampires tend to steer clear of the region. No one is quite sure why this is so, but one theory purports that garlic use in the area keeps the night prowlers at bay. A main ingredient in much of the Lowcountry cuisine, garlic is actually one of the oldest cultivated foods. In fact, the culinary, medicinal, and religious uses of garlic date back more than 6,000 years. Garlic, a natural pest deterrent, repels aphids ... and vampires. But if you spot a vampire wandering around the city, a simple garlic necklace or garlic heads placed at your windows and doors will keep the beast away. But when it comes to fending off ghosts, you're on your own.

Grilled Brace of Quail with Peanut Sauce

12	partially boned quail
1 cup	olive oil
1	small green bell pepper, chopped
⅓ cup	lime juice
1 Tbsp.	garlic, chopped
1 tsp.	parsley, chopped
1	small onion, chopped
⅓ cup	Worcestershire sauce
½ cup	brown sugar
½ tsp.	cumin
	Salt and pepper to taste
	Peanut sauce (*see below)

Combine all ingredients, except quail, for marinade. Pour over quail and chill for 4 hours. Grill quail until desired doneness. Pour peanut sauce in the bottom of the serving dish and arrange grilled quail on top of sauce.

Peanut Sauce: *

1 lb.	salted red skin peanuts (or cashews)
2 Tbsp.	vegetable oil
1 cup	chicken stock
¼ cup	cider vinegar
1	small onion, chopped
1 Tbsp.	garlic chopped
	Black pepper to taste

Purée nuts with a tablespoon of oil in food processor. Sauté onion and garlic in a tablespoon of oil, then add puréed nuts, vinegar, chicken stock, and black pepper. If sauce is too thin, you may use a teaspoon of peanut butter to thicken it.

Yield: 6 servings.

Mesquite Grilled Pulled Mallard with Apple Cider Glaze

- 4 small mallard ducks (2–3 lb.) or other mild-flavored duck
- 1 stalk celery, chopped
- 2 large onions, chopped
- Salt and pepper
- Diced lettuce
- 2 apples, quartered
- Apple Cider Glaze

Preheat oven to 350°. Clean and dress birds for roasting. Rub birds inside and out with salt and pepper. Mix celery, onion, and apples, and fill body cavity of birds with this mixture. Roast for 2 hours until brown and leg disjoints easily. Remove birds from roasting pans and cool for 30 minutes at room temperature. Remove and discard stuffing; finish cooling birds in refrigerator. Pull meat from bones, discarding bones, skin, and excess fat (this can be done the day before if ducks are not overcooked, and if meat is completely cooled, covered tightly, and refrigerated). If the grill you intend to use has large openings in the grate, leave the duck meat in larger pieces to prevent it from falling through. Grill pulled duck over coals flavored with hickory or mesquite until hot. Place on bed of washed and diced lettuce. Garnish with wedged apple and top with 1–2 ounces of apple cider glaze.

Apple Cider Glaze
- 1 gal. apple cider
- 4 Tbsp. cornstarch
- 1 stick cinnamon
- 2 Tbsp. water
- ½ orange, sliced

Place apple cider and cinnamon in a heavy non-corrosive saucepan. Boil over moderate heat until reduced to 1 pint (45–75 minutes). Add orange slices during last 5 minutes of reduction. Strain through fine sieve to remove orange and cinnamon from pot. Return cider to boil and whisk in a slurry of cornstarch and water in a slow steady stream. Stop adding cornstarch when a thick syrup consistency is reached. Keep warm until served (if sauce becomes too thick, more cider may be added).

Yield: 8 servings.

Smoked Wild Turkey

    12 lb. turkey (wild or domestic)
    2 gal. water
    1 lb. kosher salt
    1 cup olive oil
    1 Tbsp. black pepper

Soak turkey in a mixture of water and kosher salt for 2 hours. (There should be enough salt in the water to float a raw egg halfway between the waterline and the bottom of the pan.) After soaking, rub turkey with olive oil and black pepper. Place turkey on grill and cook slowly (20 minutes for each pound). Place wood chips on coals to create smoke.

                                              Yield: 12–15 servings.

No Eat-In Kitchens

Built in the 18th and 19th centuries, Charleston's many fine mansions were actually "complexes" featuring a number of outbuildings. The kitchen always occupied a separate building behind the main house because the distance helped to lessen the risk of fire to the main house, as well as eliminate the nuisance of kitchen heat, noise, and odors. Today, many of the grand homes' kitchen outbuildings have been destroyed or converted for other uses. But one historic home still stands as an intact "urban plantation." The Aiken-Rhett House, located at 48 Elizabeth Street, speaks powerfully about the culture of early Charleston. Original outbuildings include the kitchen, as well as slave quarters, stables, privies, and cattle sheds. Operated by the Historic Charleston Foundation, the Aiken-Rhett House is open for tours Monday through Saturday from 10 a.m. to 5 p.m., and Saturday from 2 to 5 p.m. Call 723-1159 for more information.

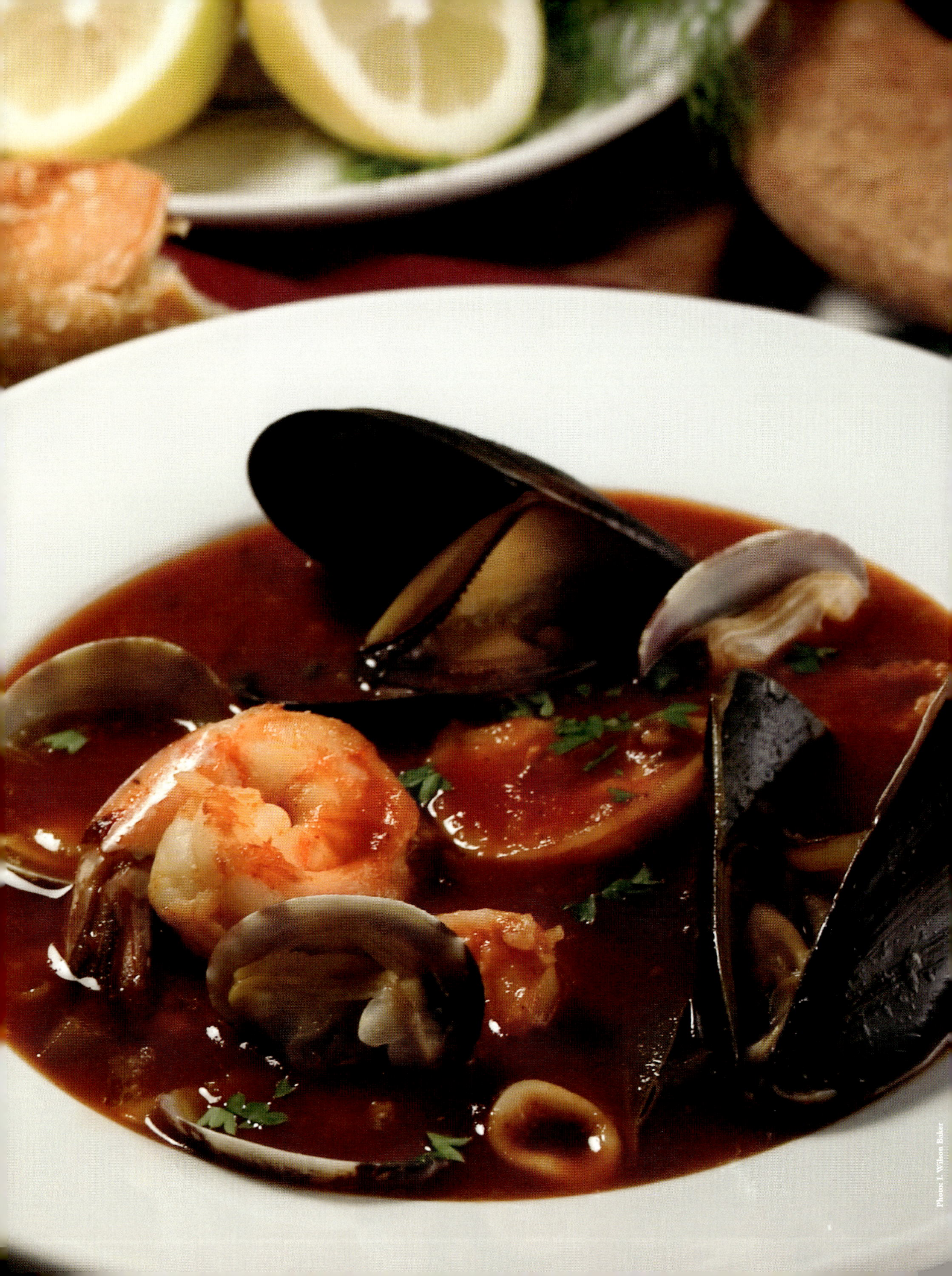

Photo: J. Wilson Baker

THE PERFECT PAIR

Lowcountry Cooking with 82 Queen

An Award-Winning Combination
Southern Wine & Spirits and 82 Queen

Providing award-winning wines for your enjoyment.

- BONNY·DOON VINEYARD
- HUGEL & FILS
- BRANCOTT VINEYARDS
- NEWTON VINEYARD
- Charles Krug — Peter Mondavi Family
- Raymond
- Columbia-Crest
- Rodney Strong Vineyards
- Francis Coppola
- SIMI — Since 1876
- Franciscan Oakville Estate
- William Hill — the taste of Central Otago since 1973

Wine and food each heighten the enjoyment of the other. When the marriage of food and wine works well, each enhances the other, making the meal greater than if you had consumed them separately. One of the most important elements of any "Pairing" is the harmony between wine and the primary ingredients of the main dish.

In "The Perfect Pair," we'll share some of our favorite Lowcountry recipes and recommend a choice of two wine selections which are sure to compliment your meal. Bon Appetite!

Grilled Beef Tenderloin with Crawfish, Leeks & Roma Tomatoes

8 (3 oz. to 4 oz.)	beef Filet Mignons
32 pieces	cooked crawfish tail meat, steamed and shelled
2 cups	leeks (washed thoroughly), cut in strips
1 cup	Roma Tomatoes, diced
1 cup	White Wine
4 Tbsp.	Basil Compound Butter (* see below)

Brush filets with canola oil, salt and pepper. After Grill has been pre-heated to a medium temperature, add filets and cook, turning at least twice. Remove fillets from grill after they reach the desired temperature. In a pre-heated medium sauté pan, add Basil Compound Butter, sauté leeks, tomatoes and crawfish for two minutes; add White Wine and simmer for two more minutes. Place filets on plates and top with crawfish mixture.

Yield: 4 servings.

Basil Compound Butter *

1/4 lb. (1 stick)	salted butter, room temperature
1/2 tsp.	Cajun spice seasoning
1 Tbsp.	fresh Basil, chopped
1/4 tsp.	garlic, chopped
1 tsp.	lemon juice
1/8 tsp.	salt

In medium size bowl, combine soft butter with other ingredients, blend well, chill, use as needed. Refrigerated and in proper container, Basil Compound Butter will last several weeks.

For the perfect wine to compliment this recipe, we recommend:

- *Rodney Strong " Knotty Vines" Zinfandel '02*
- *Franciscan Merlot, Napa '02*

Southern Wine & Spirits of South Carolina

Lowcountry Bourbon & Praline Pork Loin

4 (6 oz.)	pork loins, trimmed
8 tsp.	olive oil
8 tsp.	shallots
1 cup	pecans
2 cups	heavy cream
4 tsp.	light brown sugar
8 oz.	Bourbon
8 oz.	all purpose flour
	Salt and White Pepper to taste.

Dredge pork loins in flour, salt and pepper, set aside. Pre-heat sauté pan, add olive oil then add shallots; sauté until they turn light brown. Add pork loins, sauté for one or two minutes per side, or until golden brown. Add brown sugar and pecans to sauté pan and stir. Deglaze sauté pan with Bourbon (careful, alcohol will flame). When flame disappears reduce heat, add cream and salt and white pepper to taste. Stir gently until sauce is reduced by half (approximately three minutes), then serve.

Yield: 4 servings.

For the perfect wine to compliment this recipe, we recommend:

- *McWilliams's Shiraz, Southeastern Australia, '04*
- *Lyeth Meritage, Sonoma, California, '03*

Ben Arnold Beverage Company

Antioxidant One-Ups-Manship

We've long known that red wine contains anti-cancer compounds. But did you know that there are at least 25 antioxidants in red wine? The most celebrated of these is resveratrol, an antioxidant more powerful than Vitamin E. The resveratrol content of wine is related to the length of time the grape skins are present during the fermentation process. The concentration is significantly higher in red wine than in white wine because the skins are removed earlier during white-wine production, lessening the amount that is extracted. Two other compounds found in red wine, epicatechin and quercetin, are twice as strong as resveratrol. (By the way, wine has so many organic chemical compounds it is considered from complex than blood serum.) The U.S. Government's Center for Disease Control found that endometrial cancer (lining of the uterus) is decreased by 83% in women who consume 12 or more drinks per week. So bottoms up!

Pepper Seared Veal Tenderloins with Cranberry & Apricot Jam

8 oz.	Veal Loin cut 1 oz. medallions
1 Tbsp.	cracked black pepper
1 Tbsp.	Canola Oil
2 oz.	Grand Marnier
¼ cup	all purpose flour
	Salt to taste

Cut veal loin into eight, one oz. medallions, dredge in flour, salt and pepper, set aside. In medium sauté pan, heat Canola Oil, sear medallions one minute per side; flame with 2 oz. Grand Marnier. Arrange on plate with jam in center.

Yield: 8 servings.

Jam

8 oz.	dried cranberries
8 oz.	dried apricots (medium chopped)
1½ cup	cranberry juice
1½ cup	sugar
1 tsp.	cinnamon

Using medium size sauce pan, add all ingredients, simmer for 20 minutes, or until jam thickens, chill.

For the perfect wine to compliment this recipe, we recommend:

- *Rodney Strong Pinot Noir, Russian River '02*
- *Raymond "R. Collection" Merlot Monterey '03*

Southern Wine & Spirits of South Carolina

Berry Tales

Of the world's commercially-important fruits, only three originated in North America; blueberries, Concord-type blue grapes, and cranberries. Early Dutch and German settlers gave the cranberry its name. To them, the pink cranberry blossom resembled the head and bill of the crane, a bird that lived in the lowlands and feasted on the berries. So they called the berries "craneberries." Over time, it was shortened to cranberries.

Baked Chicken with Cornbread and Collards Stuffing and Onion Gravy over Brown Butter Rice

8 (8 oz.)	boneless and skinless chicken breasts
2	fresh cornbread muffins, crumbled
3 cups	collards, picked and thoroughly washed
1	small sweet onion (Vidalia if available), diced
1/4 lb. (1 stick)	salted butter
1	egg
1 tsp.	ground sage
	Salt and pepper to taste
8 cups	Carolina Brown Butter Rice
2 cups	Onion Gravy (*see below)

Pre-heat oven to 375° degrees; cook Carolina Brown Butter Rice according to package instructions, set aside but keep warm. Melt butter in large sauce pan. Sauté onions until transparent, then add collard greens and cook until tender. Remove from heat. In a large mixing bowl, add cooked collards, cornbread, egg and seasoning, mix and cool. Divide the stuffing mixture into eight equal portions. Stuff chicken with the skin side down. Fold and roll chicken breasts, let overlap and tuck in the ends. Place chicken on a baking pan lightly coated with cooking oil. Bake at 375° for 20 minutes or until meat is not pink when tested with a knife. Plate eight equal servings of Brown Butter Rice; cut cooked chicken breasts into an equal number of slices and arrange on top of each plate of rice, top with Onion Gravy.

Yield: 8 servings.

Onion Gravy *

2	sweet onions (Vidalia if available), julienned
2 oz.	(1/2 stick) of salted butter
3 cups	chicken stock (home-made or canned)
1 cup	Heavy Cream
½ tsp.	Kitchen Bouquet Coloring
	Black Pepper to taste
3 Tbsp.	corn starch
½ cup	cold water

In a medium size sauce pan sauté onions in butter until transparent, add the chicken stock, cream, Kitchen Bouquet and black pepper. In a small bowl, add corn starch and cold water to make a slurry, stir until dissolved. Slowly bring ingredients in sauce pan to a boil. Whisk the corn starch slurry slowly into the sauce pan, stir until the sauce is thickens.

Yield: 4 cups.

For the perfect wine to compliment this recipe, we recommend:

- *Alexander Valley Chardonnay '04 - Alexander Valley Vinyards*
- *Hanna Sauvignon Blanc '05 Sonoma*

Ben Arnold Beverage Company

Blackened Chicken with Creamy Lemon Fettuccini

4 (8 oz.)	boneless chicken breasts
1 lb.	cooked Fettuccini
30	Grape Tomatoes cut in half
1 lb.	fresh Asparagus, sliced into ½ inch lengths
2	medium/large Portabella Mushrooms, sliced vertically
1 cup	Chicken Volute (substitute Cream of Chicken Soup)
4 oz.	Chardonnay
2 oz.	lemon juice
1 Tbsp.	lemon zest
	Cajun blackening seasoning
2 oz.	Canola oil
	Salt and Pepper to taste

Season both sides of chicken with Cajun Seasoning, set aside. Pre-heat oven to 350°; cook Fettuccini pasta and set aside.

Add Canola oil to oven-proof skillet and heat to high temperature. Sear one side of each chicken breast in skillet, turning chicken over when spices begin to turn dark brown. To finish chicken, carefully place skillet in pre-heated oven for 15 minutes. While chicken is finishing, in a large pan or pot, add the remaining ingredients, except the Fettuccini. Bring ingredients to a boil; reduce and simmer for 15 minutes, stirring to a creamy consistency. Add Fettuccini to mixture and simmer another 3 to 4 minutes, season to taste.

Divide pasta mixture into 4 serving bowls and place a chicken breast on top of each serving. Garnish with Parmesan or Romano Cheese.

NOTE: If sauce becomes too thick, it can be thinned to the desired consistency with milk.

Yield: 4 servings.

For the perfect wine to compliment this recipe, we recommend:

- *Sterling Vintners Collection Chardonnay, Napa, California, '04*
- *Sonoma Cutrer RRR Chardonnay, Sonoma, California, '04*

Ben Arnold Beverage Company

Grilled Brace of Quail with Peanut Sauce

12	Quail, partially boned
1 cup	olive oil
1	small onion, chopped
1	small green pepper, chopped
1/3 cup	Worcestershire Sauce
1/3 cup	fresh lime juice
1/2 cup	brown sugar
1 Tbsp.	garlic, chopped
1 tsp.	parsley, chopped
1/2 tsp.	cumin
	Salt and Pepper to taste

In a medium size bowl, combine ingredients to make a marinade. Pour marinade over quail and chill for four hours. Pre-heat Grill to 350°, place quail on grill and sear each side. Cook until quail are no longer pink when tested with a knife. Pour peanut sauce in the bottom of the serving dish and arrange quail on top of the sauce.

Yield: 6 servings.

Peanut Sauce

1 lb.	salted Redskin Peanuts (Cashews may be substituted)
1 cup	chicken stock (home-made or canned)
1/4 cup	Apple Cider Vinegar
1	small sweet onion, chopped
1 Tbsp.	garlic, chopped
2 Tbsp.	Canola oil
	Black Pepper to taste

Puree nuts with one tablespoon of Canola oil in a food processor. In a medium size sauce pan sauté onion and garlic in one tablespoon Canola oil, then add pureed nuts, vinegar, chicken stock and black pepper.

Note: If sauce does not thicken, use a teaspoon of peanut butter to thicken sauce.

For the perfect wine to compliment this recipe, we recommend:

- *Coppola Zinfandel, Napa '03*
- *Newton Pinot Noir, Napa '02*

Southern Wine & Spirits of South Carolina

Fall Harvest Stuffed Venison Tenderloin with Bing Cherry Glaze

2 (8 oz.)	Venison tenderloins
3	cloves garlic, finely minced
1	large shallot, finely minced
½ cup	Shiitake mushrooms, thinly sliced
6	sage leaves, minced
4 oz.	Burgundy or Merlot Wine
2	slices white bread, cubed (crust removed)
2 oz.	olive oil
	Butcher's String
	Salt and Pepper to taste
	Bing Cherry Glaze (* See below)

In pre-heated sauté pan, add olive oil then add garlic and shallots, sauté until translucent; add shiitake mushrooms and sauté for one minute more. To this mixture, add wine, sage, salt and pepper, stir. Remove from heat and fold in bread cubes. Let cool to room temperature. Trim and butterfly venison tenderloins. Divide stuffing in two equal portions then place in between the butterfly-cut tenderloins. Close and tie with Butcher's String, baste with olive oil and season with salt and pepper.

Grilling Method: Preheat grill to 400°, cook venison for 5 to 8 minutes turning frequently.

Yield: 2 servings.

Bing Cherry Glaze *

1 cup	dried Bing Cherries
½ cup	Burgundy or Merlot Wine
1 cup	cranberry juice
¼ cup	brown sugar
2 tsp.	orange peel
1	orange, juiced
2 tbs.	corn starch
½ cup	cold water

In a medium size sauce pan combine ingredients (except corn starch and water), simmer 20 minutes. In a small bowl, make a slurry with corn starch. Bring ingredients to a boil. Whisk the slurry into the sauce pan and stir until the sauce has thickened slightly.

For the perfect wine to compliment this recipe, we recommend:

- *Rutherford Hill Merlot, Napa California, '02*
- *Markham Merlot, Napa, California, '03*

Ben Arnold Beverage Company

THE PERFECT PAIR 129

Sea Bass Drayton

4 (8 oz.)	Sea Bass filets
1 lb.	salted butter
1	sweet yellow pepper, julienne cut
1	sweet red pepper, julienne cut
2	fresh lemons
1 Tbsp.	fresh Thyme finely chopped (retain four sprigs)
1 Tbsp.	fresh Black Pepper, ground
8	large fresh spinach leaves* (pre-washed)
1/4 cup	all purpose flour

Lightly dust the Sea Bass filets with flour. In a good cast iron skillet, melt butter, allowing it to burn black, then add Sea Bass (it will cook quickly). When fish is seared on one side, turn over and sprinkle the dark side with fresh Thyme, Black Pepper and the lemon juice. Remove the fish from pan, allowing excess butter to drain. Plate filets on a bed of Spinach fresh leaves, garnish each with sweet peppers and a sprig of thyme on the side.

*If large spinach leaves unavailable, use 4 cups of fresh, pre-washed spinach.

Yield: 4 servings.

For the perfect wine to compliment this recipe, we recommend:

- *William Hill Chardonnay, Napa '03*
- *Coppola Chardonnay, Napa '04*

Southern Wine & Spirits of South Carolina

A Bite of History

Located on the outskirts of Charleston, Drayton Hall was built between 1738 and 1742 for John Drayton using both free and slave labor. The house stands on a 630-acre plantation that grew indigo and rice. It is the only plantation house along the Ashley River to survive the American Revolution and the Civil War intact. Seven generations of Drayton heirs have diligently preserved the original house, though the outbuildings did not survive. An earthquake destroyed the laundry house in 1886, and a hurricane destroyed the kitchen in 1893.

82 Queen Seafood Bouillabaisse

2 Tbsp.	olive oil
2½ cups	tomato stock (see recipe below)
½ lb.	fresh sea scallops
½ lb.	fresh, local shrimp, peeled and deveined
½ lb.	mussels, in shell
½ lb.	oysters, in shell
2 Tbsp.	garlic, chopped
6 to 8	spring onions, finely chopped
1 tsp.	Saffron
1½ quarts	Tomato Stock (recipe on Page 69)
½ cup	white wine
4	slices Thick Sourdough Bread (Grilled)

Prior to preparing recipe, thoroughly rinse mussels and oysters in cold water, drain on soft towel.

Pre-heat large frying pan for 30 seconds, then add olive oil. Add garlic and sauté for 30 seconds then add scallops, sauté for two minutes. Add the rest of the seafood, except oysters and cook for two more minutes. Deglaze pan with white wine then add Tomato Broth and saffron. Simmer until seafood is cooked (approximately three minutes). Add oysters last and simmer for one minute. Divide Bouillabaisse into two large serving bowls and garnish with Spring Onions. Serve with grilled sourdough bread.

Yield: 2 servings.

For the perfect wine to compliment this recipe, we recommend:

- *Brancott Sauvignon Blanc, New Zealand '03*
- *Simi "Reserve" Chardonnay, Sonoma '03*

Southern Wine & Spirits of South Carolina

French Influence

Napoleon once said, "Clearly, the pleasures wines afford are transitory, but so are those of the ballet or of a musical performance. Wine is inspiring and adds greatly to the joy of living." Spoken like a true Frenchman…and Charlestonian.

Lowcountry Crawfish or Shrimp Etouffee

1 lb.	pre-cooked crawfish tail meat or fresh local shrimp peeled and deveined
2 cups	Cajun Red Sauce (see recipe)
½ lb.	of bacon, cooked and crumbled
1 cup	celery, sliced
½ cup	onion, sliced

In a large frying pan, cook until crisp, approximately ½ lb. of bacon. Remove bacon from skillet (drain on paper towel, then crumble). Add celery and onion to bacon drippings, cook until transparent. Add Cajun Red Sauce, simmer for four minutes. To this mixture, add choice of seafood, simmer 3 to 5 minutes.
Serve hot over rice of choice.

Yield: 4 servings.

Cajun Red Sauce

¼ lb.	(1 stick) of salted butter
3 Tbsp.	all purpose flower
1 (32 oz.)	can V8 Juice
8 oz.	White Wine
¼ cup	fresh lemon juice
¼ cup	Worcestershire Sauce
1 tsp.	Cayenne Pepper
¼ cup	brown sugar
2 Tbsp.	thyme
4	Bay Leaves
1 Tbsp.	garlic, chopped
1 tsp.	Black Pepper
1 tsp.	Salt

In a large sauté pan, make roux with flour and butter. Slowly add V8 Juice and all other ingredients to roux while stirring constantly. Simmer until mixture thickens.

For the perfect wine to compliment this recipe, we recommend:

- *Conundrum, California, '04*
- *Fairview Viognier, Paarl, South Africa, '04*

Ben Arnold Beverage Company

Queen Street Frogmore Stew

1 lb.	large fresh local shrimp, peeled and deveined
1 lb.	new red potatoes
1 lb.	smoked sausage, cut into 2 inch pieces
3	ears sweet corn - husked, cleaned and quartered
1/2 lb.	fresh okra, cut in quarters
6–8	spring onions, chopped
1 1/2 quarts	Tomato Stock (recipe on Page 69)
4	slices thick Sourdough Bread (Grilled)

Pre-cook new potatoes and corn, remove from cook pot, drain. In a large stock pot, add Tomato Broth, bring to medium heat. Add new potatoes, corn, okra and sausage, cook at medium heat for 5 to 10 minutes. Stir in shrimp, cook 3 to 5 minutes or until shrimp are pink, serve immediately.

Divide Frogmore Stew into four large serving bowls and garnish with spring onions. Serve with grilled sourdough bread.

Yield: 4 servings.

For the perfect wine to compliment this recipe, we recommend:

- *Willamette Valley Vineyards Pinot Gris, Willamette Valley, Oregon, '05*

- *Hogue Gewürztraminer, Washington, '04*

Ben Arnold Beverage Company

Grilled Sea Scallops with Sweet Red Pepper Coulis with Shoestring Vegetables

20	sea scallops (20-30 count), lightly poached
2 Tbsp.	olive oil
2 oz.	Balsamic vinegar
1 Tbsp.	brown sugar
1/2 tsp.	white pepper
1/2 tsp.	Cayenne Pepper
1 tsp.	cumin
1 tsp.	chili powder
3 tsp.	Cilantro, chopped
1/2 tsp.	garlic, finely chopped
1/4 cup	water
1/2 cup	yellow squash (fine, Julianne cut)
1/2 cup	green pepper (fine, Julianne cut)
1/2 cup	red pepper (fine, Julianne cut)
	Sweet Red Pepper-Coulis (see recipe on Page 80)

In a large sauce pan, poach sea scallops in lightly salted boiling water for 2 minutes, drain and set aside. In a medium size bowl, add all ingredients, except scallops; mix well using a whisk. To the mixture add poached scallops and set aside for a minimum of 30 minutes (room temperature).

Shoestring Vegetables: Pre-cook cut squash, green pepper and red pepper in a medium size pot of salted, boiling water for one minute. Remove and strain vegetables, then transfer to ice water bath. Drain thoroughly and set aside.

Preheat Grill to 350°, sear scallops, one minute per side. Evenly divide Sweet Red Pepper Coulis into six shallow serving bowls. Arrange five scallops in each bowl, top with Shoestring Vegetables; garnish with fresh chopped Cilantro.

Yield: 4 servings.

For the perfect wine to compliment this recipe, we recommend:

- *Charles Krug Sauvignon Blanc, Napa '04*
- *Columbia Crest Chardonnay, Washington State '03*

Southern Wine & Spirits of South Carolina

Mesquite Grilled-Citrus Glazed Mako Shark with Sour Cream and Herb Sauce

4 (7 oz.)	Mako Shark steaks
1/2 cup	concentrated orange juice
1/4 cup	fresh lemon juice
1/4 cup	fresh lime juice
2 Tbsp.	fresh thyme
1 cup	sour cream
2 Tbsp.	Tarragon Vinegar
1 tsp.	fresh thyme
1 tsp.	fresh oregano
1 tsp.	fresh basil
2 dashes	Tabasco
	Salt and White Pepper to taste

In a covered bowl in the refrigerator, marinate shark steaks in mixture of orange juice, lemon juice, lime juice and fresh thyme for at least two hours. Chop thyme, oregano and basil and add to sour cream. Using a Wisk, blend tarragon vinegar and Tabasco with the sour cream mixture, seasoning to taste. Chill at least two hours. After Grill has been pre-heated to 350°, add wet mesquite chips to coals allowing them to burn for five minutes. Cook shark steaks four minutes per side. Place grilled shark steak on a plate, top with the sour cream-herb sauce.

Yield: 4 servings.

For the perfect wine to compliment this recipe, we recommend:

- *Chalk Hill Sauvignon Blanc, Sonoma, California, '03*
- *Alexander Valley Vineyards Chardonnay, Alexander Valley, California, '04*

Ben Arnold Beverage Company

Puppy Chow

The largest Mako shark on record weighed in at 1,207 lbs. It was caught by angler Jodie Daniels on March 2, 1990 off the coast of Kona, Hawaii. But that big fish seemed like a pup (the correct term for a baby shark) compared to the 3,450 lb. Great White pulled from the Atlantic Ocean by Don Braddick on August 6, 1986.

Shrimp & Andouille Sausage with Creamy Grits

30 - 40	local shrimp, peeled and deveined
1 lb.	Andouille Sausage, sliced into rings
3 - 4	leeks (thoroughly washed) and cut into small rings
2	sweet red peppers
1/4 cup	Cajun butter (* see below)
	Salt and White Pepper to taste
	Creamy Grits (** see below)

Sauté leeks and Andouille Sausage for one minute in Cajun Butter. Add shrimp and red peppers, cook another two minutes or until shrimp are done (they turn pink). Season with salt and pepper and serve over grits.

Yield: 6-8 servings.

Cajun Butter *

1 lb.	salted butter
1/8 cup	Cajun Seasoning
2 Tbsp.	lemon juice
2 Tbsp.	tomato paste
1 Tbsp.	red Tabasco sauce
1 Tbsp.	granulated garlic
1 Tbsp.	granulated onion

To butter softened at room temperature (about an hour), add remaining ingredients. Mix thoroughly until all ingredients are incorporated. Use as needed. Refrigerated and in proper container, Cajun Butter will last several weeks.

Creamy Grits **

2 cups	water
1 cup	of quick grits
2 cups	heavy cream
1/4 lb.	(1 stick) salted butter
1 tsp.	salt
1/2 tsp.	White Pepper

Add quick grits to boiling ingredients; simmer for 20 minutes stirring often.

For the perfect wine to compliment this recipe, we recommend:

- *Willamette Valley Pinot Noir, Willamette Valley, Oregon, 2003*
- *Markham Merlot, Napa, California, 2003*

Ben Arnold Beverage Company

Grilled Shrimp and Proscuitto with Brie Cheese Sauce

16	jumbo shrimp, peeled and deveined (30 count)
1/2 cup	olive oil
1/4 cup	White Wine
1/4 cup	fresh lemon juice
1/4 cup	fresh basil
1 tsp.	garlic, finely chopped
1 tsp.	sugar
1/2 lb.	Proscuitto Ham
2	fresh lemons
2 (heaping) cups	of Red-Veined Spinach
1/4 cup	toasted Pinenuts
	Salt and White Pepper to taste

Peel, devein, clean and rinse shrimp. In a medium size bowl, mix olive oil, white wine, lemon juice, chopped basil and chopped garlic, add shrimp and marinade and refrigerate for at least two hours. Slice Proscuitto into 16 very thin slices (one inch wide and three inches long). Cut fresh lemons in 12 wedges. Wrap Proscuitto around shrimp and put four wrapped shrimp on a skewer alternating with lemon wedges. Preheat Grill to 350° then add wet mesquite chips to coals. Allow chips to smolder for 5 minutes. Place shrimp skewers on Grill, turning often and basting with marinade during grilling. Serve the shrimp on a bed of spinach. Top with Brie cheese sauce and toasted Pinenuts.

Yields: 2 servings.

Brie Cheese Sauce

2 oz.	(1/2 stick) of salted butter
2 Tbsp.	all purpose flour
8 oz.	Brie Cheese (crust removed)
1	pint milk
2 dashes	Tabasco Sauce
	Salt and White Pepper to taste

In a medium size sauté pan, make roux with flour and butter, slowly add milk and whisk. After mixture begins to thicken, add brie cheese and seasoning while stirring constantly.

For the perfect wine to compliment this recipe, we recommend:

- *Ca Donini Pinot Grigio, Italy '04*
- *Hugel Pinot Blanc, Alsace, France '04*

Southern Wine & Spirits of South Carolina

Yellowfin Tuna with Fresh Mozzarella over Saffron Risotto with Wakame Salad and Blood Orange Vinaigrette

4 (8 oz.)	Yellowfin tuna filets
4	(1/2 inch) pieces of Mozzarella Cheese
1/2	medium size onion, diced
2 Tbsp.	Canola Oil.
1 cup	Arborio Rice
2 cups	chicken stock (homemade or in a can)
1 tsp.	Saffron
1/2 cup	heavy cream
1 Tbsp.	salted butter
1/4 cup	Parmesan Cheese
	Wakame Salad*
	Blood Orange Vinaigrette (recipe Page 33).

Pre-heat (high) large black skillet, sear tuna quickly on both sides (rare). Place tuna on a broiler tray and top with fresh, sliced Mozzarella Cheese, set aside until Risotto is cooked.

In a large, pre-heated frying pan, add Canola oil heat, add onion, sauté until translucent. Add uncooked Arborio Rice to pan and coat in oil and onion mixture. Add chicken stock 1 cup at a time, stirring constantly until rice absorbs all stock (about 20 minutes). Note: Saffron should be added with first cup of chicken stock. After rice has absorbed all the chicken stock, stir in heavy cream, butter and cheese. Put tray with tuna and Mozzarella Cheese under a pre-heated broiler for approximately 30 seconds (possibly 1 minute, depending on tray's distance from heat). Serve tuna over the Risotto, top with Wakame Salad* dressed with a Blood Orange Vinaigrette.

Yield: 4 servings.

*Wakame Salad can be purchased in the Sushi section of most high end grocery stores. If unavailable, substitute steamed spinach.

For the perfect wine to compliment this recipe, we recommend:

- *William Hill Chardonnay, Napa '03*
- *Rodney Strong Pinot Noir, Russian River '04*

Southern Wine & Spirits of South Carolina

BANANA SPLIT CHEESECAKE

4 (8 oz.)	packets of softened cream cheese (room temperature, one hour)
4 oz.	light brown sugar
1/4 lb. (1 stick)	butter, softened (room temperature, one hour)
2 cups	graham cracker crumbs
1 cup	sugar
2 Tbsp.	vanilla extract
4 Tbsp.	cornstarch
2	large bananas, mashed
5	large eggs

Mix brown sugar, butter and graham cracker crumbs together and press firmly into the bottom of a 9" Spring Form pan. In a large mixing bowl, add cream cheese, sugar, vanilla and cornstarch, blend well with a hand mixer. Add eggs to mixture and blend well. Add mashed bananas to mixture, blend well again. Pour mixture into the Spring Form pan. Bake at 325° for 65 minutes. Cool several hours in refrigerator until set. Remove Spring Form pan from cheesecake. Serve with strawberries, chocolate sauce, whip cream and chopped nuts.

Yield: 1 Cake.

For the perfect wine to compliment this recipe, we recommend:

- *Domaine de Coyeaux Muscat de Beaune de Venise*

Southern Wine & Spirits of South Carolina

Dessert, Anyone?

There are only three legal categories of wine in the United States: table, dessert and sparkling. In the early 1950s about 82% of all wine consumed by Americans was classified as dessert wine, including Sherry, Port and Maderia. Things have certainly changed over the more than half century. Today about 90% of all wine Americans drink is classified as table wine, with sparkling wine consumption at 7% and dessert wine consumption at a mere 3%

Holiday Cranberry Bread

2 cups	all purpose flour, unbleached
1/2 cup	sugar
1 Tbsp.	baking powder
1/2 tsp.	Salt
2/3 cup	fresh orange juice
2	Eggs
3 Tbsp.	salted butter
1/2 cup	Walnuts, shelled and coarsely chopped
1 1/4 cup	cranberries, fresh
2 tsp.	orange rind, grated

Preheat oven to 350°. Grease an 8 x 4 1/2 x 3 inch bread pan.

Sift flour, sugar, baking powder and salt into a mixing bowl. Make a well in the middle of the sifted mixture and pour in orange juice, eggs and melted butter. Stir well without over mixing. Fold in walnuts, cranberries and orange rind. Pour batter into the prepared pan and set on the middle rack of the oven.

Bake for 45 to 50 minutes or until a knife inserted in the center comes out clean. Remove bread from the oven and cool in the pan for ten minutes, then remove bread from pan and allow to cool completely on rack. Wrap and put away for one to two days before serving.

Yield: 1 loaf.

For the perfect wine to compliment this recipe, we recommend:

- *Biltmore Estate White Zinfandel, North Carolina*
- *Trim Bach Riesling, Alsace, France, '03*

Southern Wine & Spirits of South Carolina

Double Chocolate Ganache Cheesecake

1 1/2 cup	Oreo Cookies (about 18 cookies), crushed
1/4 lb.(1 stick)	butter, softened (room temperature)
1 (12 oz.)	package semi-sweet chocolate morsels
3 (8 oz.)	packages cream cheese, softened
1 (14 oz.)	can sweetened condensed milk
2 tsp.	vanilla extract
4	large eggs
	Ganache Topping (* see below)

Pre-heat oven 300°. Crush cookies in Zip-Loc bag with rolling pin. Add softened butter and cookie crumbs in a bowl, mix well. Press cookie crumbs into bottom and halfway up sides of a 9-inch Spring Form pan; set aside.

In a glass bowl, microwave chocolate morsels at HIGH for 90 seconds or until melted, stirring at 30-second intervals. In a large bowl, whip softened cream cheese (medium speed) with electric mixer 2 minutes, or until smooth. To the cream cheese, add sweetened condensed milk and vanilla, beating at low speed just until combined; add eggs, one at a time, beating at low speed just until combined after each addition. Add melted chocolate, beating just until combined. Pour cheesecake mixture into prepared crust.

Bake cheesecake in 300° oven for 1 hour 5 minutes, or just until center is set. Turn oven off. Let cheesecake stand in oven 30 minutes with oven door closed. Remove cheesecake from oven; run a knife along outer edge of pan, cool in pan on a wire rack until room temperature. Cover and chill 8 hours.

Remove sides of Spring Form pan and place cake on a serving plate. Slowly pour and spread warm Ganache Topping over top of cheesecake, letting it run down sides of cheesecake. Chill 1 hour before serving.

Yield: 8–10 servings.

Ganache Topping *

3/4 cup	whipping cream
1 (6 oz.)	package semisweet chocolate morsels (1 cup)
1 (6 oz.)	package milk chocolate morsels (1 cup)

In a sauce pan, slowly bring cream to a boil over medium heat, stirring constantly. Quickly remove pan from heat, stir in semi-sweet and milk chocolate morsels until melted and smooth. Before pouring and spreading over cheesecake, let mixture cool (slightly warm) about 30 minutes.

For the perfect wine to compliment this recipe, we recommend:

- *Domaine de Coyeux Muscat de Beaune de Venise*
- *Bonny Doon Vin de Glaciere*

Southern Wine & Spirits of South Carolina

Heart Healthy Lemon Cheesecake

2 Tbsp.	Mazola light spread
1/4 cup	graham cracker crumbs
1 cup	oatmeal
1/2 cup	brown sugar
20 oz.	Light and Lively fat-free cottage cheese
8 oz.	light cream cheese (Neufchatel cheese)
6	egg whites
2 Tbsp.	lemon juice
1/2 cup	sugar
	Topping (* see below)

Combine Mazola, graham cracker crumbs, oatmeal, and brown sugar in a mixing bowl and pack into the bottom of a 9-inch springform pan. Bake for 18 minutes at 350°. Combine cottage cheese, cream cheese, egg whites, lemon juice, and sugar in a bowl and mix with an electric mixer until smooth. Pour over the crust in the springform pan and bake 40 minutes at 325°. Pour topping over cheesecake while still in pan, before the cheesecake has cooled. Chill for 3–4 hours in the refrigerator before removing from the pan.

Topping *

8 oz.	Light and Lively sour cream alternative
1 tsp.	sugar
2 tsp.	lemon juice

Mix all ingredients well.

Yield: 12–16 servings.
149 calories, 4 1/2 g. fat, 14 mg. cholesterol, and 246mg. sodium.

For the perfect wine to compliment this recipe, we recommend:

- *Jekel Riesling*

Ben Arnold Beverage Company

Wining and Dieting

Need to shed a few pounds? Did you know that wine is a significant aid in the treatment of obesity? Studies show that dieters who drink a 4 to 5 ounce glass of dry wine at dinner or bedtime lose twice as much weight as dieters in control groups who don't. Interestingly, dry wine is also effective in the treatment anorexia, a condition characterized by excessive weight loss. One explanation for this paradox may be that the wine helps alleviate anxiety and emotional tension associated with both obesity and anorexia.

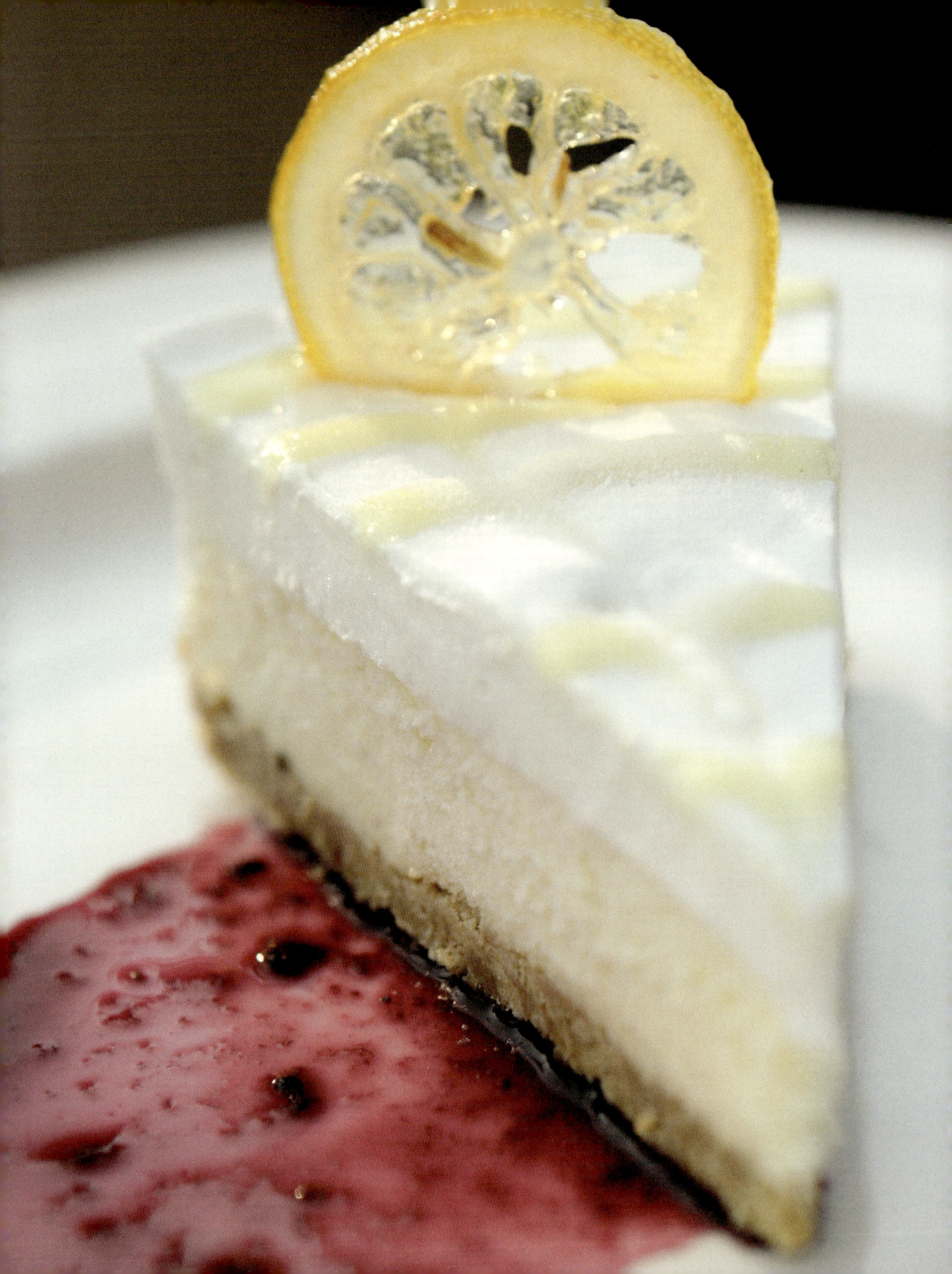

Desserts

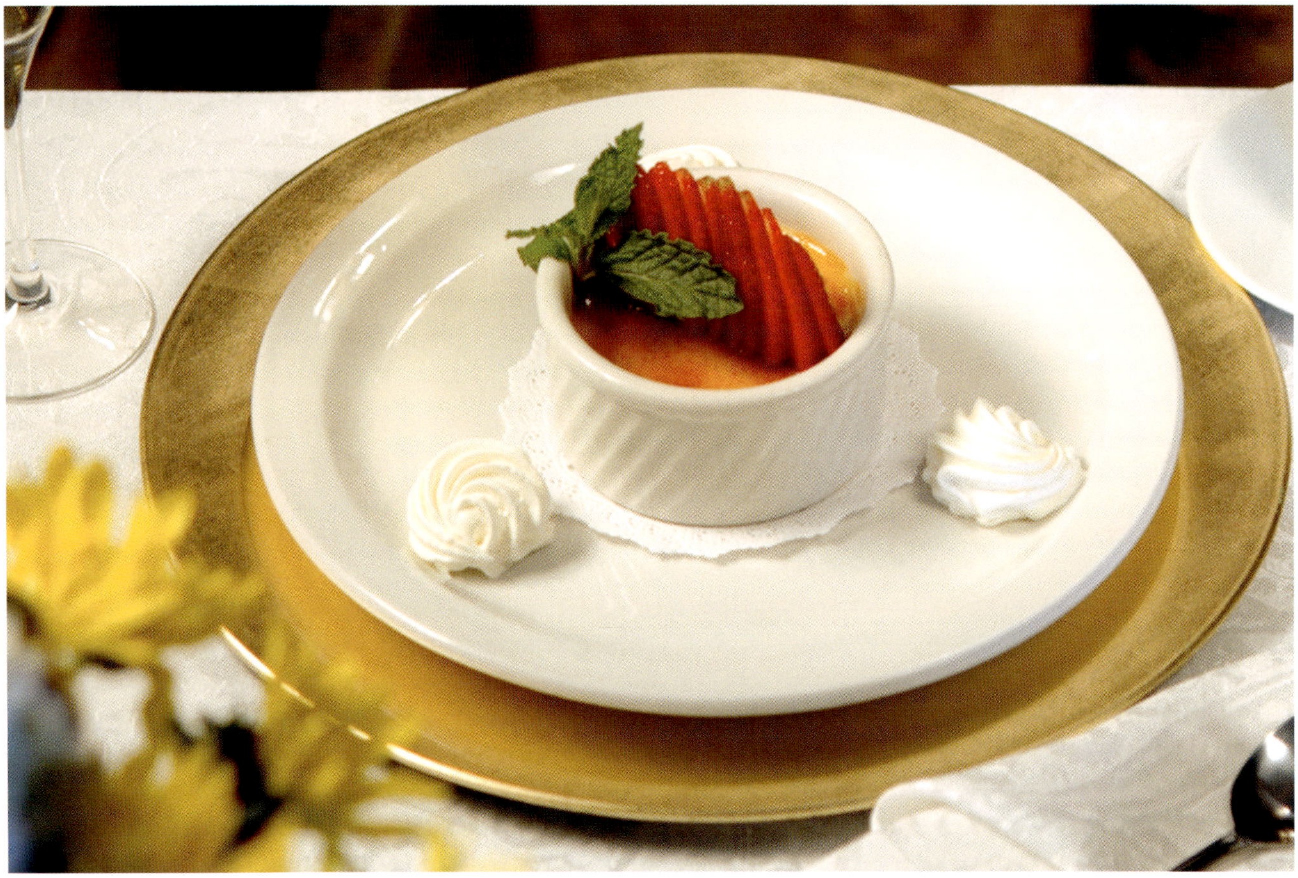

Photo: I. Wilson Baker

Desserts

Angel Pie ... 148

Apple Spice Cake with Carmel Sauce ... 149

Autumn Fruit Pie ... 150

Bananas Foster ... 150

Blueberry Nut Pie ... 151

Chocolate Caramel Cheesecake ... 151

Chocolate Raspberry Cheesecake ... 152

Crème Brûlée ... 152

Crème Anglaise ... 153

Death by Chocolate ... 153

Graham Cracker Crust ... 154

Hazlenut & White Chocolate Mousse ... 155

Key Lime Pie ... 156

Lemon Chess Pie ... 157

Peach Praline Cobbler ... 158

Pecan Pie ... 159

Pumpkin Marble Cheesecake ... 160

Raspberry Swirl Cheesecake ... 161

Strawberry Banana Pie ... 162

Toll House Pie ... 163

Angel Pie

3	egg whites
1 cup	sugar
1 tsp.	baking powder
1 cup	chocolate wafers, chopped fine
1 tsp.	vanilla
1 cup	pecans, chopped
1/2 cup	whipped cream

Beat egg whites and vanilla to form soft peaks while gradually adding sugar, beating until stiff peaks form. Mix nuts, wafer crumbs, and baking powder. Fold in beaten whites and spread evenly in greased, floured 9-inch pie pan. Bake at 325° for 20–25 minutes. Cool completely and top with cream.

Yield: 1 pie.

Just Peachy

Georgia may be the called "The Peach State," but South Carolina is "The Tastier Peach State." South Carolina has a long heritage of peach production which from the 1860s. But today peaches are grown in three main regions of the state – the "Ridge," which is in the south central area; the "Coastal Plain," which runs along the eastern shore; and the "Piedmont," which runs along the northwest region of the state. There are about 35 varieties and 200 million pound of peaches harvested in South Carolina annually. In fact, South Carolina ranks second in fresh peach production and interstate shipments. (By the way, "The Peach State" ranks third nationally in fresh production. At one time, ONE COUNTY in South Carolina produced more commercially-grown fresh peaches than the entire state of Georgia.)

Apple Spice Cake with Caramel Sauce

³/₄ cup	pecan halves (2 1/2 oz.)	¹/₈ tsp.	ground cloves
³/₄ cup	raisins	¹/₈ tsp.	mace
¹/₄ cup	bourbon	2 cups	sugar
1 cup	cake flour	1 cup	vegetable oil
1¹/₂ tsp.	baking soda	1 cup	all-purpose flour
¹/₂ tsp.	salt	2	eggs
¹/₂ tsp.	fresh ground nutmeg	2	large Granny Smith apples unpeeled and diced (3¹/₂ cup)
¹/₂ tsp.	cinnamon		Caramel Sauce (* see below)

Preheat oven to 400°. Spread the pecans on a baking sheet and toast in the middle of the oven for about 5 minutes, until fragrant and golden brown. Chop coarsely and set aside. Reduce the oven temperature to 325°. In a small bowl, combine the raisins and bourbon and set aside to macerate for 30 minutes. Butter and flour a 10 x 3-inch springform pan. In a medium bowl, sift together the cake flour, all-purpose flour, baking soda, salt, nutmeg, cinnamon, cloves, and mace. Set aside. In a large bowl, using an electric mixer, beat the sugar and vegetable oil at medium speed for 5 minutes. Add the eggs one at a time, beating well after each addition. Add the dry ingredients all at once and stir with a wooden spoon until thoroughly incorporated; the batter will be very thick. Drain the raisins. Using a spatula, stir them into the batter along with the diced apples and toasted pecans until well distributed. Scrape the batter into the prepared pan and bake for 1–1¹/₂ hours, or until a knife inserted in the center comes out clean. Transfer the pan to a rack to cool slightly, then turn the cake out of the pan and let cool completely. Drizzle cake with caramel sauce.

Caramel Sauce *

1 cup	heavy cream
1 cup	dark brown sugar
¹/₃ cup	granulated sugar
¹/₄ cup	pure maple syrup
¹/₄ cup	light corn syrup

In a heavy saucepan, stir together all the ingredients until thoroughly combined. Cook over high heat until the mixture reaches 210° on a candy thermometer. Set aside to cool for 20 minutes. The sauce can be made up to 3 days ahead; transfer to an airtight container and refrigerate. Reheat over warm water or in a microwave oven.

Yield: 8 servings.

Autumn Fruit Pie

1	half-baked, 9-inch, deep-dish pie crust
	Filling (* see below)
	Topping (** see below)

Arrange filling in pie crust and sprinkle topping on top. Bake at 325° for about 1 hour.

Filling *

2	large apples, peeled and pared
2	large pears, peeled and pared
6 oz.	fresh cranberries
1 cup	sugar
3 Tbsp.	flour
1 tsp.	cinnamon

In a large bowl, combine ingredients and mix well.

Topping **

3 Tbsp.	butter or margarine, slightly melted
1/2 cup	quick cooking oatmeal
1/2 tsp.	cinnamon
1/2 cup	brown sugar, packed
1/2 cup	flour

Mix ingredients with pastry blender until crumbly. Add a little more flour if it looks wet.

Yield: 8 servings.

Bananas Foster

1	banana, cut into strips
2 Tbsp.	butter
1 oz.	dark rum
1 Tbsp.	light brown sugar
1/2	fresh orange, juiced

In saucepan, melt butter and sugar. Add banana sections and sauté 1 minute. Turn over and add rum and juice from orange. Serve over ice cream.

Yield: 1 serving.

Blueberry Nut Pie

2	pre-baked pie shells
8 oz.	pkg. cream cheese, room temperature
2 cups	walnuts
3/4 lb.	powdered sugar
1 (21 oz.)	can blueberry pie filling

Blend cream cheese and powdered sugar; place in baked shells. Sprinkle chopped nuts on cream cheese, then divide blueberries on top. Top with whipped cream and nuts.

Yield: 2 pies.

Chocolate Caramel Cheesecake

1 2/3 cups	graham cracker crumbs
5 Tbsp.	margarine, melted
1	(14 oz.) bag Kraft caramels
1 cup	pecans, toasted and chopped
1 tsp.	vanilla
2 (8 oz.)	pkgs. cream cheese, softened
1/2 cup	semi-sweet chocolate pieces, melted
1 (5 oz.)	can evaporated milk
1/2 cup	sugar
2	eggs

Preheat oven to 400°. Spread the pecans on a baking sheet and toast in the middle of the oven for about 5 minutes until fragrant and golden brown. Combine graham cracker crumbs and margarine and press with back of spoon onto bottom of 9-inch springform pan. Bake at 325° for 5 minutes. In 1 1/2-quart saucepan, melt caramels with milk over low heat, stirring frequently until smooth. Pour over crust. Top evenly with pecans. Combine cream cheese, sugar, and vanilla, mixing at medium speed on electric mixer until well blended. Add eggs and mix well. Blend in melted chocolate and mix again. Scrape sides and mix again. Pour over pecans. Bake at 325° for 35–40 minutes (middle will set as it cools). Cool in refrigerator several hours before removing from pan.

Yield: 12 servings.

Chocolate Raspberry Cheesecake

1 3/4 cups	crushed Oreo-type cookie crumbs
2 Tbsp.	melted margarine
4 (8 oz.)	bricks cream cheese, slightly softened
1 1/2 cups	all-purpose flour
1 tsp.	vanilla
1 (12 oz.)	jar raspberry jam (seedless)
1 cup	sugar
1 tsp.	lemon juice
4	eggs

Mix cookie crumbs and margarine well and press smoothly onto the bottom of a 10-inch springform pan. Bake at 325° for 8 minutes and set aside to cool. In a large mixing bowl, add sugar, flour, vanilla, and lemon juice to slightly softened cream cheese. Mix well until blended. Add eggs and mix again until well blended. Add the jar of jam and mix well again. Pour into crust and bake at 325° for 45 minutes. Cool on counter at least 30 minutes, then in refrigerator for at least 5 hours before removing from pan. Serve over bed of chocolate sauce.

Yield: 12 servings.

Crème Brûlée

4 cups (1 qt.)	heavy cream
1	vanilla bean or 2 tsp. vanilla
	Pinch of salt
8	egg yolks
3/4 cup	sugar
8 tsp.	brown sugar

Heat heavy cream, salt, and vanilla until it begins to skim over (5 minutes). Cream together egg yolks and sugar, then add cream mixture. Try to avoid bubbles. Strain mixture if necessary. Fill ramekin to the rim. Place in pan and add water to bath. Cover with foil. Bake at 300° for 1 hour or until firm around the edge. Chill for 2 hours. Top with brown sugar and broil until sugar melts.

Yield: 8 servings.

Crème Anglaise
Serve on Death by Chocolate or cobbler, or as a base for cheesecake

4 cups	heavy cream
1 tsp.	salt
9	egg yolks, beaten lightly
3/4 cup	sugar
3 tsp.	vanilla
1 Tbsp.	brandy

Combine cream and sugar in a double boiler; stir until sugar is dissolved. Bring up to not quite scorching heat. In a bowl, combine eggs, vanilla, brandy, and salt. Mix well. Add a little of the warm cream mixture and whisk together. Pour this mixture into the double boiler of cream. With a wooden spoon, vigorously stir together over medium heat. Slowly continue to stir in a figure-eight motion until it thickens. Remove from heat and allow to cool down in a separate container to room temperature, then refrigerate.

Yield: 16 servings.

Death by Chocolate

1/2	box light brown sugar
4 Tbsp.	margarine, melted
1 cup	graham cracker crumbs
2	sticks butter
1 Tbsp.	vanilla
18 oz.	semi-sweet chocolate chips, melted
1/2	box powdered sugar
6	extra large eggs

Combine margarine, graham cracker crumbs, and brown sugar. Mix well and press in the bottom of a 9-inch springform pan. Bake at 325° for 8 minutes and cool. In large bowl, soften butter slightly in microwave (about a third or half-melted) for 2 minutes on low power. Using electric mixer, combine softened butter with powdered sugar and vanilla. Melt chocolate chips in microwave in separate bowl until consistency is smooth. Pour into butter mixture and mix well. Then add eggs, 3 at a time, mixing well. Pour into crust and bake at 350° for 20 minutes. Cool in refrigerator about 6 hours before cutting from pan.

Yield: 12 servings.

Peach Praline Cobbler

   2 (16 oz.) bags frozen sliced peaches
1½ cups self-rising flour
  1 cup of milk
1½ cups sugar
   2 extra large eggs, beaten
     Topping (*see below)

Thaw peaches in the refrigerator. Place the thawed peaches in a bowl and add ¼ cup sugar and sprinkle with cinnamon. Set aside. Strain off the excess juice. Combine flour, milk, sugar and beaten eggs; mix well and pour into bottom of well-greased 9 x 13-inch metal pan. Arrange the peaches on top of the batter evenly. Sprinkle evenly with topping. Bake at 350° for 70 minutes.

Topping *
  1 cup self-rising flour
1½ cups pecans, chopped coarsely
  ½ box light brown sugar
  ½ stick margarine, room temperature

In a small bowl, cut margarine into small pieces and soften by using a serving spoon like a pastry blender. Mix in a portion of the other ingredients until crumbly. Do this for a few minutes, then put aside. Repeat this step several times until all ingredients are combined.

Yield: 12 servings.

Pecan Pie

4	eggs, extra large
1 cup	white sugar
1 cup	dark Karo syrup
1½ tsp.	vanilla
2 Tbsp.	bourbon (or to taste)
2 Tbsp.	melted butter
2 cups	pecan pieces

Beat eggs and white sugar. Add remaining ingredients. Pour into pie shell and bake 1 hour 10 minutes at 325° or until firm.

Yield: 1 pie.

Pumpkin Marble Cheesecake

1 1/4 cup	ginger snap cookie crumbs
1/4 cup	pecans, chopped fine
1/4 cup	margarine, melted
2 (8 oz.)	pkgs. cream cheese, slightly softened
3/4 cup	sugar
3	eggs
1 tsp.	cinnamon
1 tsp.	vanilla
1 cup	canned pumpkin
1/4 tsp.	ground nutmeg

Combine ginger snap crumbs, pecans, and margarine and press flat on bottom of 9-inch springform pan. Bake at 325° for 10 minutes. Combine cream cheese, 1/4 cup sugar, and vanilla, mixing until well blended. Add eggs, mixing well. In another bowl, mix 1 cup cream cheese batter, remaining sugar, pumpkin, and spices. Alternately layer pumpkin and cream cheese batters over crust. Cut through layers with knife several times for marble effect. Bake at 325° for 55 minutes. Allow to cool several hours in refrigerator before removing pan.

Yield: 12 servings.

Raspberry Swirl Cheesecake

1 1/2 cup	graham cracker crumbs
1/2 cup	sugar
4 Tbsp.	butter
4 (8 oz.)	pkgs. cream cheese
4	eggs
2 Tbsp.	vanilla
4 Tbsp.	seedless raspberry jelly, melted to a liquid
1/2 cup	flour
2 Tbsp.	lemon juice
14 oz.	sweet condensed milk

Melt butter. Add graham cracker crumbs and sugar to butter, mixing well. Spread on bottom of 10-inch springform pan until flat. Set aside. In large bowl, soften cream cheese in microwave (about 4–5 minutes on medium heat). With electric mixer, blend cream cheese and flour. Add eggs and mix well. Add vanilla, lemon juice, and milk. Pour 1/3 cheesecake mixture into springform pan. Drizzle 1/3 of the liquid jelly on top, then the next 1/3 cheesecake and again with the jelly, repeating until all mixtures are gone. Swirl with butter knife so the jelly will swirl in the cheesecake. Bake at 300° for 35 minutes. When you take it out of the oven, it will not look completely done; it firms up as it cools. Cool for at least 6 hours. After several hours in the refrigerator, the cheesecake can be removed from the pan. Slice and serve with a raspberry sauce.

Yield: 12 servings.

Strawberry Banana Pie

5 oz.	powdered sugar
1 pt.	fresh strawberries
1/4 cup	walnuts, chopped
1	graham cracker pie crust
4 oz.	cream cheese
1	banana
1/2 cup	whipped cream

Mix cream cheese and powdered sugar together with a hand mixer until fluffy. Spread mixture on the bottom of the pie crust. Chill for 10 minutes. Slice strawberries and banana and layer them on top of the cream cheese mixture. Top with whipped cream and sprinkle chopped walnuts over pie.

Yield: 1 pie.

Toll House Pie

2	eggs
1/2 cup	sugar
1 cup	walnuts, chopped
1 cup	butter, melted and cooled to room temperature
1 cup	(6-oz. pkg.) Nestle semi-sweet real chocolate morsels
1/2 cup	unsifted flour
1/2 cup	brown sugar, packed
1 (9-inch)	unbaked pie shell

Preheat oven to 325°. In large bowl, beat eggs until foamy; beat in flour, sugar, and brown sugar until well blended. Blend in melted butter and stir in Nestle morsels and walnuts. Pour into pie shell. Bake at 325° for 1 hour. Remove from oven. Serve warm with whipped cream or ice cream. Garnish with whole walnuts, if desired.

Yield: 1 pie.

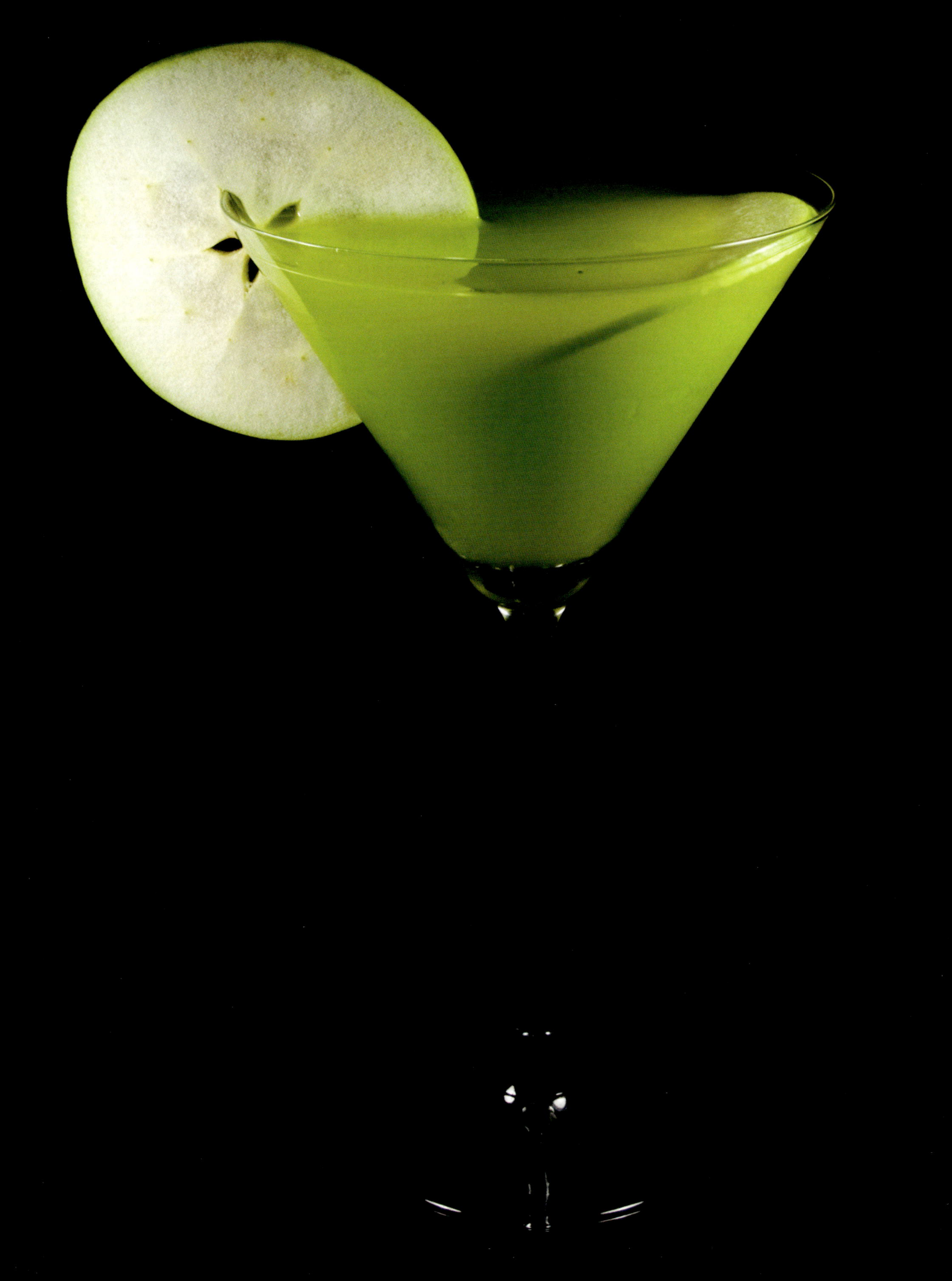

# COCKTAILS

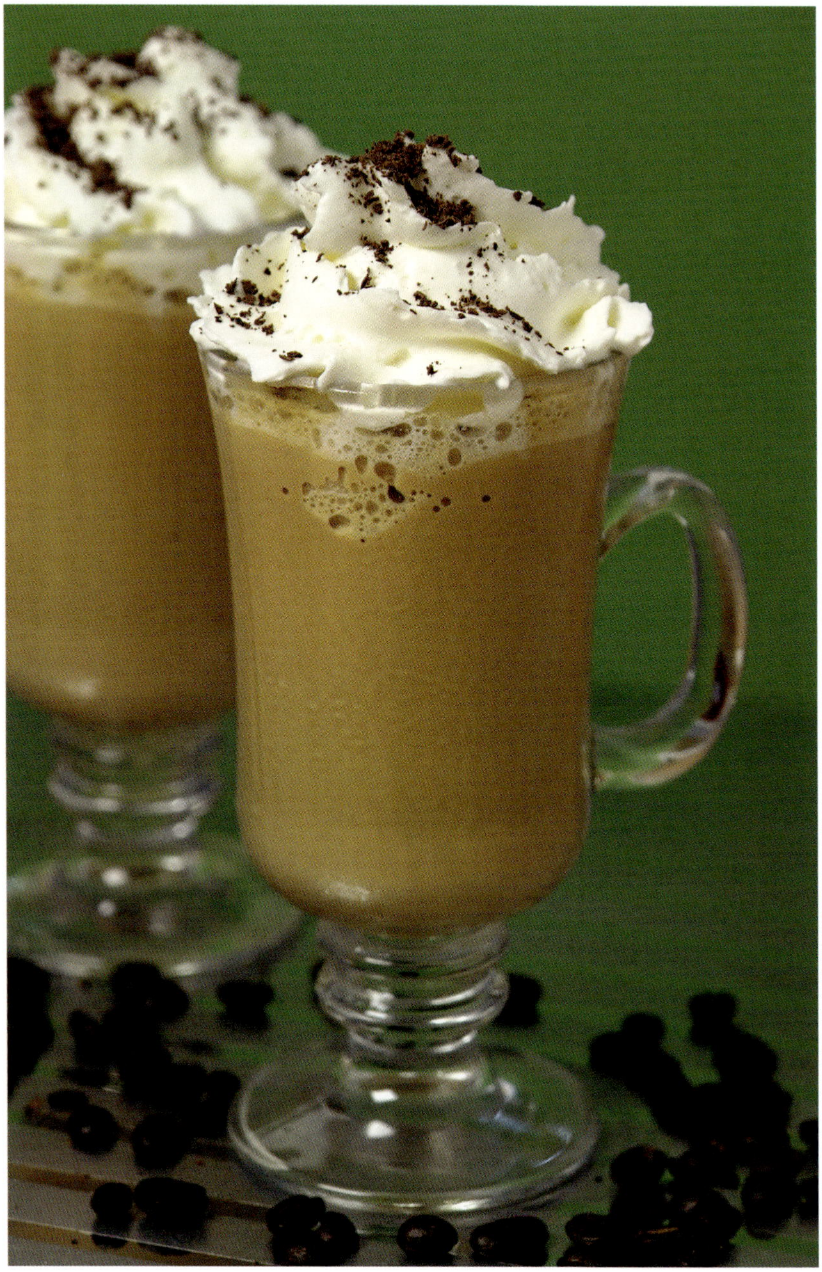

COCKTAILS

82 Queen Award-Winning Bloody Mary ... 169

82 Queen Charleston Lemonade ... 169

82 Queen Cosmopolitan ... 169

82 Queen Mint Julep ... 170

82 Queen Margarita ... 170

Brandy Alexander ... 170

Christmas Eggnog ... 171

Godiva Chocolate Martini ... 171

Queen Street Spritzer ... 171

EXCELLENCE
from the Historic City

Enjoy these Lowcountry Originals...

- Amber
- Pale Ale
- Porter
- Charleston Lager

PALMETTO BREWERY
289 Huger Street, Charleston, South Carolina

82 Queen Award-Winning Bloody Mary

24 oz.	vodka
1	can tomato juice
1	can V-8 or 82 Queen Bloody Mary Mix
8–10 dashes	Tabasco sauce
1/3 cup	Worcestershire sauce
1/3 cup	lemon juice
1/3 cup	horseradish
4–5 dashes	coarsely ground black pepper
1–2 dashes	celery salt
1–2 dashes	olive juice
1–2 dashes	onion juice

Combine ingredients and shake well. Pour into glass and garnish with boiled shrimp and lemon or lime.

Yield: 12 servings.

82 Queen Charleston Lemonade

1 3/4 oz.	vodka
5 oz.	homemade lemonade
1 oz.	cranberry juice

Fill a 14-oz. glass with ice. Add vodka, lemonade and cranberry juice. Garnish with a fresh lemon slice.

Yield: 1 drink.

82 Queen Cosmopolitan

1 oz.	vodka
1/2 oz.	cranberry juice
1/4 oz.	Rose's lime juice
1/4 oz.	triple sec

Shake ingredients together thoroughly and serve garnished with a lemon twist.

Yield: 1 drink.

82 Queen Mint Julep

	Crushed ice
3	sprigs fresh mint
1 teaspoon	superfine sugar
1 3/4 oz.	Kentucky bourbon
1 dash	club soda

Muddle mint and sugar in an 8-oz. glass. Fill with crushed ice. Add bourbon and a dash of club soda. Garnish with a sprig of mint.

Yield: 1 drink.

82 Queen Margarita

1 oz.	Jose Cuervo Gold tequila
1/2 oz.	Grand Marnier
4 oz.	sour mix
1/2 oz.	Rose's lime juice
1/4 oz.	triple sec
1/2 oz.	orange juice

Shake all ingredients together (for frozen Margarita, add ice and frappé in blender until smooth). Pour into glass rimmed in salt and garnish with lime slice.

Yield: 1 drink.

Brandy Alexander

1 cup	vanilla ice cream
1 oz.	brandy
1 oz.	cream

Mix ingredients in blender. Pour into glass and sprinkle with cinnamon.

Yield: 1 drink.

Mint Julep: An Intoxicating Blend

While browsing Charleston's antiques district, you might be fortunate enough to discover a proper silver julep cup. Why a special silver cup just for serving mint juleps? Silver speaks of a Southern family's traditions and wealth, while mint is considered a symbol of hospitality. The blending of the two inspires the ideal image of a genteel Southern gathering. While silver julep cups have been replaced by glass in recent years, mint juleps still require a special presentation. Made from sugar, water, Kentucky bourbon, and fresh mint, their aroma and taste still embody the hospitality that is uniquely Southern.

Christmas Eggnog

12	egg yolks
3/4 cup	sugar
1 cup	dark rum or bourbon
12	egg whites, beaten stiffly
2 cups	milk
1/2 tsp.	nutmeg
1	pinch of salt

Whip together egg yolks, salt, and sugar. Slowly add rum and milk. Fold in egg whites and nutmeg. Chill and serve.

Yield: 3–5 servings.

Godiva Chocolate Martini

1 oz.	vodka
1 oz.	Godiva chocolate liqueur
1 oz.	cocoa
1 oz.	sugar

Mix vodka and liqueur over ice and shake. Pour into glass rimmed with cocoa and sugar mixture.

Yield: 1 drink.

Queen Street Spritzer

1	bottle champagne
3 cups	cranapple juice
1	lemon
1	lime

Combine champagne and cranapple juice and pour into glasses. Garnish with lemon and lime slices.

Yield: 8–10 servings.

"Popped" Culture

Contrary to popular belief, Dom Pérignon did not invent champagne. However, the 17th-century cellar master of the Abbey of Hautvillers greatly improved the bottling process. By using thicker bottles and tying the cork down with string, Pérignon was able to prevent the champagne bottles form exploding. Pérignon is also celebrated for developing the art of blending wines to create champagnes with superior flavor. For the record, true champagnes with superior flavor. For the record, true champagne comes from France's Champagne region, located 90 miles northeast of Paris.

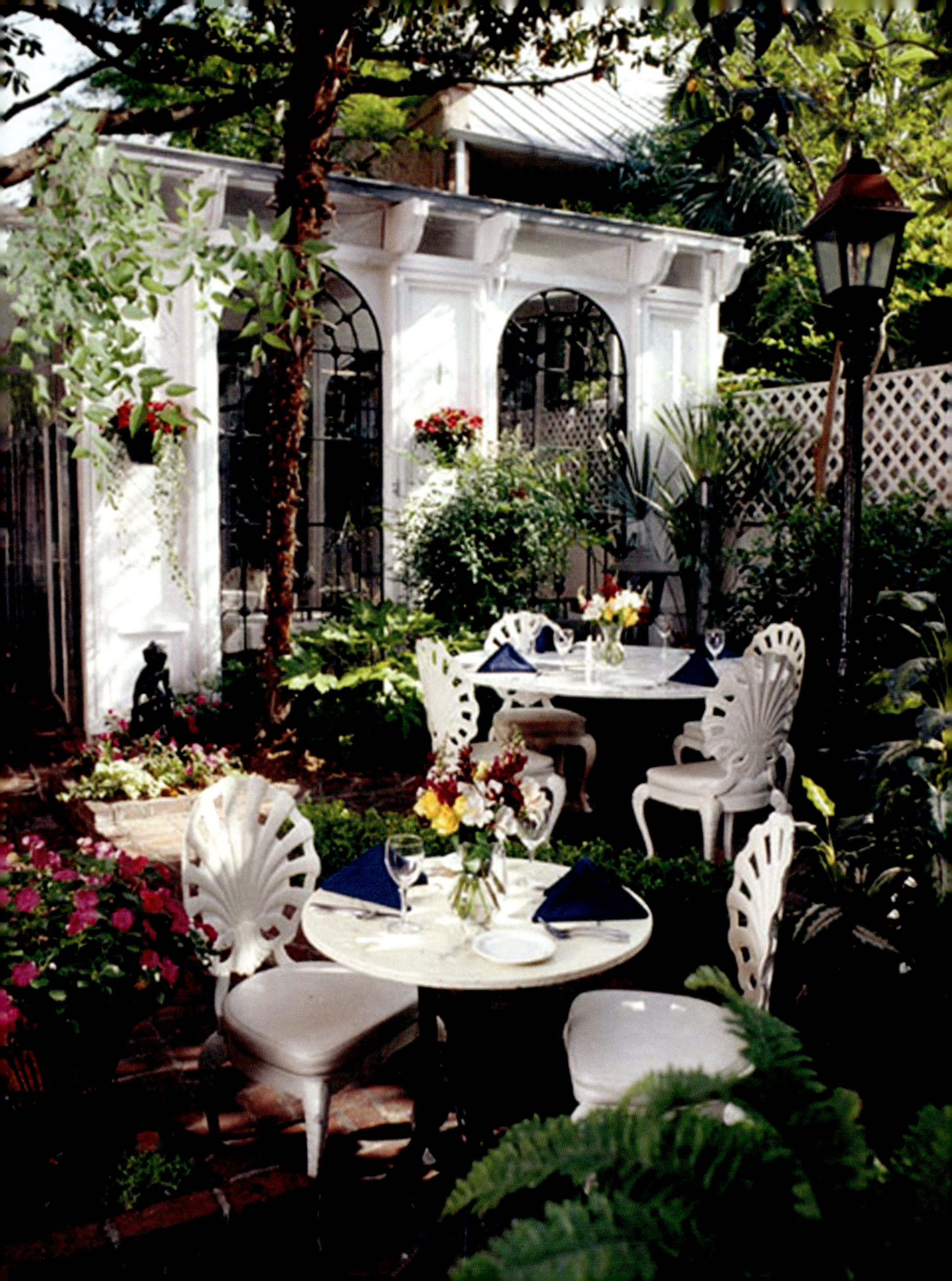

CONDIMENTS & MERCHANDISE

Lowcountry Cooking with 82 Queen

82 Queen Merchandise & Condiments

Lowcountry Cooking with 82 Queen ... 176
Lowcountry BBQ Sauce ... 176
Lowcountry Grits ... 177
82 Queen She-Crab Soup Mix ... 177
Small 82 Queen Gift Basket ... 177
82 Queen Lowcountry Seasoning Mix ... 178
82 Queen Bloody Mary Mix ... 178
82 Queen Sportsman Cap ... 179
82 Queen Short Sleeve T-Shirt ... 179
82 Queen Short Sleeve Golf Shirt ... 179

Lowcountry Cooking with 82 Queen

The cookbook shares the best and most frequently requested menu selections of 82 Queen. This labor of love reflects the desire of the owners and staff at 82 Queen to share their recipes for the best Lowcountry cuisine in Charleston. Recipes include: Award Winning She Crab Soup, Shrimp Gazpacho, BBQ Shrimp & Grits, Daufuskie Deviled Crab, McClellanville Crab Cakes, Oyster Gumbo, Toogoodoo Vegetables & Shrimp in Parchment Paper; featuring "The Perfect Pair."

$24.95

Lowcountry BBQ Sauce

Ingredients; tomato concentrate, onion, bacon, vinegar (cider and sugar), mustard, Worcestershire sauce, pepper, salt, distilled bourbon liqueur, natural flavoring.

$6.50 per 12 oz bottle

82 Queen Stone Ground Grits

Old-fashioned, South Carolina creamy stone-ground grits.

$6.00 per 10 oz can

82 Queen She-Crab Soup Mix

Just add a little cream, water, and she crab to our She Crab Soup Mix and you'll be able to enjoy some of Charleston's best She Crab Soup, right in your own home.

$6.00 per 6 oz can

Small 82 Queen Gift Basket

Includes 82 Queen BBQ Sauce, 82 Queen Creamy Grits, BBQ Shrimp & Grits Recipe, She Crab Soup Mix.

$20.00 per basket

82 Queen
Lowcountry Seasonings

A delightful mix of Lowcountry seasonings, used daily by the chefs at 82 Queen. Enhances flavor of chicken, pork, steak or seafood.

$5.00 per 6 oz bottle

82 Queen Bloody Mary Mix

A blend of tomato juice, lime juice, horseradish, Lowcountry spices, and dill. Just add vodka. Enjoy.

$7.00 per bottle

82 Queen Sportsman Cap

All cotton, wide bill, adjustable sportsman caps. Available in a wide variety of colors.

$15.00 per cap

82 Queen Short Sleeve T-Shirt

Available in Small, Medium, Large, Extra Large and XX Large. Wide variety of colors from which to choose.

$15.00 per shirt

82 Queen Short Sleeve Golf Shirt

Available in Small, Medium, Large, Extra Large and XX Large. Wide variety of colors from which to choose.

$40.00 per shirt

Stop by our website often for new products and merchandise!

— www.82queen.com —

Patra Taylor Bucher, Contributing Writer

The colorful commentary of local writer, Patra Taylor is featured in *Lowcountry Cooking with 82 Queen*. A freelance writer for 16 years, her articles have appeared in a number of prestigious publications including Charleston's *Post & Courier*, *Charleston Magazine*, American Airlines' in-flight magazine, *Latitudes*, *MD News*, *Carolina Homes & Interiors*, and *Coastal Condo Living*. Patra is a regular humorist and features correspondent for *The Charleston Mercury*. She is also the local editor and features writer for *Discover Charleston* and *Connoisseur: The Magazine of Kiawah Island Golf Resort,* upscale destination publications produced by HCP/Aboard Publishing, a division of Knight-Ridder Newspapers. *Discover Charleston* and its sister publications showcase Patra's ability to tell a rich, gripping stories. These elegant, four-color, visitor guides can be found in 9,640 of the area's best inns, resorts, and hotel rooms. Married with three children, this native of Ohio has lived in the Charleston area since 1985.